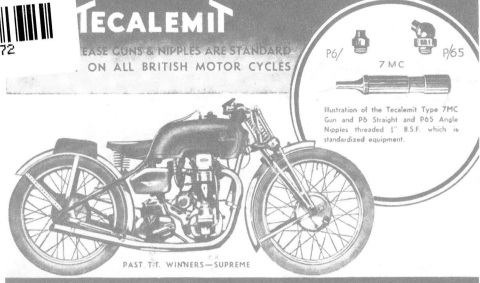

An Old Motor Kaleidoscope of
MOTOR CYCLING

By
Dennis Howard

PUBLISHED BY
OLD MOTOR MAGAZINE
17 AIR STREET LONDON W1

THE AUTHOR

DENNIS HOWARD has been fascinated by motorcycles and motorcycling for longer than he cares to admit. His first clear recollection 'sometime around 1930' is of directing two Brough Superior riders from the Savernake Forest to the London Road. He remembers their riders as 'bright young chaps in plus-fours, suede jerkins and hatless, yet wearing gauntlets and goggles to show their serious intent'.

In the mid-thirties Dennis acquired his own first bike, a touring Rudge of venerable age, which to ride 'was sheer elixir'. No one dreamt of owning a car; a bike was the only way for an impecunious enthusiast with shorts, Aertex shirt and pack to travel. And travel he did - all over the country, to trials, race meetings, and anywhere else that motorcyclists gathered.

After doing his bit for King and Country his yearning for bikes from the twenties led him to a 1927 Scott Super Squirrel 498cc two speeder. Without realising it, he was a founder member of the post-war vintage movement, even dressing the part with his breeches, stockings and plug pouch. In the late forties he joined *The Motor Cycle* under Arthur Bourne, or as he was known to his followers, Torrens - a great believer in individual freedom who would ride his Ariel Square Four to the Houses of Parliament at the slightest hint of anti-motorcycling bureaucracy. Dennis Howard learned much from him, which he has effectively put to use as President of the Motorcycle Action Group in their recent campaign against the compulsory wearing of crash hats. He is not against helmets as such, he simply feels that it is up to the individual to decide whether to wear one or not.

At *The Motor Cycle* Dennis did a bit of everything. He loved road racing and once rode 150 miles non-stop to cover a meeting at Cadwell Park on a motor-assisted bicycle that was replenished from cider bottles full of petroil carried in his jacket! Unfortunately, he found trials at the time a bit boring, and when he wrote and said so, he was attacked from all quarters! A suggestion that there ought to be a vintage TT found more support, but led to trouble from the top when he contacted old riders without asking his employers' permission. This led to an amicable parting of the ways and wider experience of the industry for Dennis Howard. He joined Tandon, and worked in several departments before taking over as salesman from Jack Troughton, the intrepid Francis-Barnett rider of the twenties, who was finding trips to Tandon dealers around the country too cold and uncomfortable at his age. Dennis continued to write about motorcycles and is today one of the leading freelance experts on the subject. He took up competitive riding in the late fifties with a Scott Sprint Special which he admired at Royston Hill Climb and acquired for a modest £25.

Nowadays he takes part in dozens of events, either as rider or commentator, and writes regular articles on our once great motorcycle industry for *OLD MOTOR MAGAZINE*. He is disappointed with current trends in motorcycling, hoping that the 'grossness of the so-called superbikes and pre-occupation with the sport may give way to more of the old camaraderie that used to exist between riders'. He says that choosing the pictures for this *OLD MOTOR KALEIDOSCOPE* helped him to recapture much of the old atmosphere and hopes that readers will enjoy sharing the pleasure that was his in its preparation.

FOREWORD

SHOULD IT be a crime to look back on motorcycling life through rose tinted goggles, then let me (oh please, please!) plead guilty on every possible count. Yes, of course, there were those occasional moments of doubt, of heartbreak, of bleak despair. After all, have I been the only one to crouch forlornly on a 5.30am garage forecourt, out of petrol, and with no chance of any before 9 o'clock? To pobble home carefully from an outing to Shrewsbury, the pillion passenger operating what remained of a broken clutch cable? To squat, swearing, under a Gloucester railway bridge while trying to mop winter floodwater from the contact-breaker of a coil-ignition Model S Royal Enfield? Probably yes; but virtually every reader could no doubt quote experiences equally as harrowing.

What the heck, anyway. It was all a part of growing up, and the blank days were more than compensated for by countless happy hours. Remember that feeling of glowing pride, when your 150cc Excelsior Villiers managed to struggle, two-up, to the very top of Ankerdine Hill, without you having to slip the clutch except on the very steepest bit? And the anxiety with which you kicked over the engine, the first time you had carried out a decoke all by yourself; followed by the overwhelming relief of hearing it fire immediately? Then there were the unimaginable thrills - like the time you were standing at the very apex of Melbourne Corner when Crasher White came hurtling down the hill at the head of the pack, and lived up to his name by arriving at your feet, minus machine. (When *was* that, anyway? Late summer of 1938, I think.)

But about this book. To a very large degree, Dennis Howard's world is akin to my own, and here, through the eye of the contemporary camera, he carries us back to times that were more leisurely and, indeed, more peculiarly innocent than those of today. So, as you turn on the water drip of the acetylene generator and wait for the smell, go on and have a good old wallow in nostalgia. I'm going to, anyway ......!

BOB CURRIE

Published by: Old Motor Magazine
17 Air Street
London, W.1.
Proprietor: Prince Marshall
UK Registration: 1453244

Designed by: Brian Harris

Printed by: Blackwell's, Oxford.

SALUTE TO THE PIONEERS

It is now more than seventy years since a remarkable number of men chose to push the crude motor bicycle and indeed themselves to a point where quite extraordinary tests of both reliability and endurance were undertaken with more than a prayer's width of confidence.
The author gained most vital knowledge of the pioneer period and its characters, having had the fortune to meet one of its 'greats', Canon B H Davies [*Ixion* of *The Motor Cycle*] in later years at his Oxfordshire home.
The discussions were rich, so much so that one was left pondering the question, what had not been attempted.
We must certainly be aware that we should not be riding the fine motorcycles of today had it not been for the salty fellows of yesteryear who, armed most times with both brain and brawn, made the motorcycle.
Consider, as we confidently travel our modern highway, by contrast the Great North Road on a filthy night in times long past as the true pioneer went his way.

1   Far, far from all the tragic happenings at Hilldrop Crescent, Camden Town and Hawley Harvey Crippen, some young men of 1910 rode fast motor bicycles in the Isle of Man.
   Our happy picture shows a bunch of racers standing by their machines, following a practice session. In the immediate foreground stands a German NSU, while the sleek racer in the centre is a BAT [Best After Test], manufactured in Penge, S E London, its creators being well established competitors at Brooklands. Personalities from left to right are Percy Butler, who retired at Peel on the first lap during the actual TT, Harry Reed, another retirement when his belt pulley fractured, H H Bowen, who fell at Creg Willeys and broke his frame. More disastrous matters affected F W Dayrell's continuation, when the head of his rear cylinder blew off. W H Bashall, standing immediately behind the BAT, experienced fire at St Johns, his machine being entirely burnt out. Brother Bashall, J T, retired also, as did the little fellow G E Stanley who already wears more than a philosophical air about him

Blue Riband of the Sunbeam MCC's veteran motorcycle activities is the annual Pioneer Run from Epsom Downs [Tattenham Corner] to Brighton, for motorcycles manufactured up to 1914. First staged in 1930, the event attracts what I like to consider real enthusiasts both as riders and spectators. Prior to 1939, the start was often organised along the Portsmouth Road, where we see a certain Mr Cook, possibly the very gentleman who held Brooklands' high speed records in its very earliest years, about to set off on his 1914 550cc Triumph in 1936. On this occasion the gallant gentleman was celebrating his 73rd birthday.

Not in any way an authority on veteran motorcycles, I might possibly question, however, the type of forks as fitted to Mr Cook's machine, which surely only appeared on Triumph machines after 1914. More familiar in veteran years were the famous 'back and forwards' barrel spring variety front suspension items

3 As mentioned elsewhere in this album, veterans are hardly my domain. I do, of course, respect that without them we should never have been able to enjoy the machines of our own very special periods of motorcycling enjoyment. Perhaps the engineer in me finds offensive the very crudity of these pioneer devices. Early aircraft, ships and locomotives were somehow never quite as bad.

This water-cooled device is a Humber Olympia Carrier Tricar, with all-chain drive and a massive power unit in inclined position, made under licence from Joah Pheton [the P of P&M]. The scene is *circa* 1904

Some idea of road conditions at this period may be gained from the state of the mudguard section. A posted Archibald remains immaculate, however

4 11th July 1919 and E J 'Cannonball' Baker raises the dust as he slides his Indian, during heavy cross-country going. Intent on regaining the 'Three Flags' record, which entailed riding from Canada to Mexico, a distance of 1714 miles, in the shortest possible time, Baker encountered the terrible hazard of deep mud in the first section of the 'race', although creditably covered the distance of 137 miles between Blaine and Seattle in 2 hours 55 minutes. This would necessitate near TT average speeds, as one observer wrote at the time. Ironically, Cannonball was delayed by engine trouble at Bakersfield for 5½ hours, yet completed the total mileage of the competition in 59 hours 47 minutes, thus becoming once more 'Three Flags' Champion. Note electric lighting

5 To achieve world acclaim, following his flight from Newfoundland to Ireland, with aviation partner Arthur Whitton Brown during 1919, this picture was taken when our subject was just Pilot J Alcock, RN. Later, both men were to receive knighthoods for their courageous transatlantic crossing in a Vickers Vimy. Already a very experienced aviator, Alcock had taken third place in the London-Manchester-London flight during the pre-Kaiser War days. An enthusiastic motorcyclist - and somehow flying and motorcycling always went wing in saddle in their own special way - Pilot Alcock is seen sitting on his 1914 TT model Douglas. Best described as rather 'sweet' little bikes, the horizontally opposed twin cylinder motors possessed more or less sewing machine rhythm in their going. At this period, the two speed gearbox was placed beneath the rear cylinder, while gear operation was made by the quadrant assembly mounted on the tank top, the actuating lever passing through it. The large pipe, forming a 'bow' above the flywheel, is all part of the induction system, most times efficient although a tricky item for good carburation on a wintry day

[*Above*] **Highgate, London, N6, in all its
~~~ber glory, June 1919, and the assembly of
~~mpetitors prior to the London-Edinburgh
~~un.**

In the foreground will be seen perhaps one
~~ the most revolutionary motorcycles of the
~~y, the Wooler, affectionately referred to as
~~e 'Flying Banana' as its fuel tank extended
~~rward of the steering head, somewhat in the
~~ape of that West Indian fruit.

Possessing very advanced features, the
~~ooler - named after its brilliant engineer
~~eator John - could boast of full plunger
~~spension for both front and rear wheels, and
~~ginally a two-stroke engine where crank-
~~se compression was not necessary to action
~~e two stroke cycle. By 1920, horizontally
~~posed twin cylinder engines [350cc] with
~~et over exhaust valve arrangement had
~~laced the single cylinder two stroke unit,
~~hough the distinctive shape of Wooler
~~torcycles continued right up until the finish
~~production in the mid 1950's

7 [*Left*] **Strict formality being the order of
the day, members young and old of the
Uxbridge Cycling Club are seen checking the
weight of a competing motorcycle in events
organised by the club. The picture was taken
in 1903, when the new sport of motorcycling
took over to some degree from cycling,
although it was to be a time before true
motorcycling clubs came into being.** Interesting is the trim little machine standing on the
weighing platform, for already it had been
appreciated that the traditionally high riding
position for cycling with a saddle way in the
air was far from suitable when the device
would be required to corner at twice the speed
now under power, hence the 'new' saddle
position as shown here. The scoreboard in the
background would indicate that the event was
some type of gymkhana mixed with a little
high speed stuff around the field perimeter.
Things are being taken very seriously!

8 [*Above*] It could just be that the line-up of competitors for the Auto Cycle Club's [later ACU] fuel consumption test of 1905 are standing with their machines outside *The Flask* public house at Highgate. Much motorcycling activity took place in the South of England during these early years, with often a test course extending through St Albans, Redbourn and on to the Northamptonshire border. More or less in the centre stands the famous pioneer motorcyclist, Pa Applebee [cigarette in mouth], with his Rex machine, while to the left of this fine picture is surely Charles Jarrott in semi-military cap. Along with the two forecars appears a typical example of the sporting tricycle, no doubt of De Dion make. The motor bicycle on the extreme left has been worked on by its owner

to a fine art where the fuel tank proper missing, no doubt to reduce unnecessa weight

8A Worn proudly on the watchchain many a grand fellow who made it in th England/Scotland run, the famous Mote Cycling Club's 'gold'. Clearly evident in th engraving feature is St Paul's Cathedral symbol of the City of London, and Edinburg Castle marking the northern end of affair Sadly, all the substance went out of this MC event when war came along in 1914

9 [*Left*] That interesting period about the very early years of this century, before the sidecar became accepted practice for a sociable journey with one's sweetie.

No easy situation in starting procedure: consider the rider of this Kelecom-engined machine, who would be obliged to pedal with some vigour while the motorcycle remained on its stand, and at the same time operate several controls on the tank top area until the engine fired. The remaining action was a masterpiece of handling. Rugged types, on the other hand, might well have chosen to pedal into motion in forward direction, the weighty assembly 'dropping' the exhaust valve lifter at an appropriate moment. Amid the exhaust fumes would Alice issue a few words of sympathy to our now perspiring Clarence!

10 [*Above*] **Line-up for the 1913 Senior TT.** One can nearly smell the hot road, oil, petrol and the seasoned leathers of the riders. Pushing off is Oscar Godfrey on a 500cc Indian, now shorn of its forwardly inclined other cylinder. Simply, a plate was bolted over the crankcase mouth, the remaining cylinder equally inclined rearward, which gave the machine a rather odd appearance. In this particular event, Godfrey retired. Other marques in evidence are Rudge-Multi [97], so named as it possessed a variable gear which could register approximately sixteen different ratios. Number 96 is a standard Triumph TT model, with the familiar barrel spring, fore and aft fork movement. Ensuring that there shall be no risk of missing a swift gear change, Rover entrant number 98 appears to have made sufficient leverage on the change speed lever, upon which he has his left hand. 1913 was the last year in which the leather flying helmet was permitted, for in the following year crash hats were compulsory, although some competitors here would appear to have precipitated this!

Split into a two-day event for 1913, the race was eventually won by Tim Wood riding a Scott machine

11 [*Left*] **Mr Dot himself, or rather Harry Reed,** Managing Director of the original Manchester based DOT Company - no complication to the letters DOT, merely initials for the words Devoid of Trouble! The potent piece of battleware is interesting, for Reed had won the twin cylinder class of the 1908 TT with a 680cc inlet over exhaust Peugeot engined device, later using V twin side valve JAP units, right up until 1914. The DOT in this pre-Kaiser War picture clearly shows that it has an overhead valve V twin engine and such is the position of the rockers that it is for sure that the valves were vertically positioned in their respective cylinder heads. I would suggest that the picture was posed prior to, or just after some Northern speed event when Reed may well have been experimenting with overhead valve JAP engines. The bald front tyre reminds me of an incident some years ago when a local policeman, coming upon a band of enthusiasts with well-worn tyres, remarked, 'If there was not so much unemployment about I would book the lot of you!' Strange that so many of these pioneer types rode on tyres shorn of any tread pattern at all!

12 Of remarkably advanced design, the Paul Kelecom brainchild, the Belgian FN straight four, provided somewhat luxurious motor-cycling in the early years. Consider that such models existed in 1904, their first appearance being made at the Paris Salon in that year while variations on the general theme continued until 1923.

The original FN had automatic inlet valves and fully enclosed shaft and bevel drive in the transmission department and was rated at 3hp. Note the interesting bottom link spring forks.

The gentleman seated on his 1909 model here is a brother of the late Percy Preston, proprietor of the Holly Park Garage, Regents Park Road, Finchley. Being a master tailor, it can be appreciated why he favoured such a mechanically clean machine

13 At the bottom of this page we have an artist's impression of Charlie Collier engaged on his epic ride while, *right*, Collier is seen at the conclusion of the record. A contemporary report of this high speed canter stated that neither Collier brother [H A being the other Matchless Company partner] showed any sign of pleasure when all was done, the reason being that some days beforehand C R had lost one to two in a series of three match races against the great American rider Jake de Rosier [Indian] at Brooklands. Thus, in its way, if an 'after run', at least Collier had made the fastest ever on that sultry August Friday evening 65 years ago.

The red Matchless was fitted with JAP engine No 10516, Amac carburettor, Bosch magneto, Hutchinson tyres and Gloria belt. Lubricant by Vacuum and petrol by Pratts

14 'Made like a Gun' was the original sales slogan for the Redditch, Worcestershire made Royal Enfield. In the later years of the thirties, and indeed during the post-war period, one usually associated the Enfield with trials and scrambles motorcycles and a more than ample range of 'bread and butter' machines.

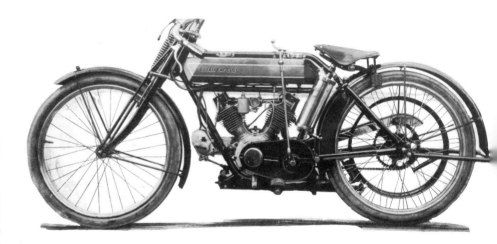

Dainty would be the most appropriate word to describe the 1914 TT model shown here however, with its 350cc V twin engine and inlet over exhaust valve system. Two additionally interesting features were the two-speed gear operating lever, running from tank top to primary chain case housing, and the clear glass oil tank situated on the seat pillar tube. Eight, of nine machines entered in the '14 Junior TT, completed the distance, although rider F J Walker, who was a certainty for third place at the conclusion of the race, crashed into a barrier a short distance from the finishing line and later died from his injuries. He was awarded third place posthumously

15 Readers of *OLD MOTOR* will recall the very interesting article by P J Wallace about his motorcycling experiences prior to the First World War, and how the very idols of his period had been the Collier brothers, manufacturers of Matchless motorcycles at Plumstead. Perhaps Mr Wallace had even stood atop the mighty Brooklands banking in 1911 and viewed in awe the exploits of Charlie Collier as he hurtled round the concrete saucer on the 8hp Matchless-JAP. Since that glorious time, however, the world's fastest motorcycle speeds have risen to well over 200 mph, although we should never forget Pioneer Collier's fantastic speed on what we would now consider a more than flimsy device

16 I recall the time when the dashing Harry Martin was referred to as the Edwardian Geoff Duke by journalists of the motorcycle press. Martin will always be associated with Excelsior motorcycles, as a rider of the marque for many years, and in later times as designer and consultant. I suspect that this picture of Harry, posing a racing crouch for photographer Campbell-Gray, was taken at the Canning Town race track sometime in 1903. The Excelsior machine, manufactured by Bayliss, Thomas and Company of Coventry must be described as pretty basic with a huge 400cc MMC engine literally clipped to the front down tube of a reinforced bicycle frame. The large plated tube on the offside of the model is the induction pipe from carburettor to the automatic inlet valve. On such an Excelsior the first measured mile was covered in just under 60 seconds at Phoenix Park, Dublin, in 1903

17 Although not particularly attracted to veteran motorcycles, in this case, however, the Triumph is categorised as very early vintage - being a 1915 model - if the day is right and my mood is right a very definite enjoyment can be derived from taking saddle on such a machine. Of course, the whole exercise is thoroughly spoilt when one is obliged to wear a safety helmet to do it in, which destroys a very vital moment of atmosphere as well as vulgarising such a gentle pursuit. Quite in order that over Flanders' fields the Don R of the Kaiser War years would ride his Trusty Model H Triumph, but with a service cap upon a gallant head. Possibly the most famous of war heroes where motorcycles are under review during 'The First Lot', the side valve Trusty with its chain cum belt transmission and barrel spring front forks which moved backwards and forwards rather than up and down under shock will be remembered with nostalgia by many a gentleman now in the autumn of his life

18 The Rudge Multi, so called as its variable gear could offer a considerable number of ratios. This picture, taken in 1914, will give some idea of the system of operation. The long vertical lever, just by the rider's left knee, directly actioned the inner flange of the crankshaft mounted pulley by means of a four lobed cam plate, which in turn worked against cam surfaces formed on the outer crankcase cheek. The large rear wheel pulley was also provided with separate flanges, the inner one being fixed to the wheel rim, while its mate was spoked to a splined sleeve, sliding inside the hub. This flange was connected by an assortment of rods and levers to the gear lever and cam plate. If the gear lever was moved backwards, low ratios were obtained, as the rear wheel pulley closed and the engine pulley opened by belt pressure. To raise the gear, the lever would be moved forward, belt pressure then opening the rear pulley, and the cam plate closing the flanges of the engine pulley. All perhaps a little Gerard Hoffnung, in one way or another, but just the cat's pyjamas for our pipe smoking sporty boy fifty years ago

The begining to Road Racing

Prelude to the world's greatest motorcycle road races - the TT event. High speed competition on powered two wheelers
in any organised form worthy of mention were the series of races first run in 1904 in France.
Originally called the International Motorcycle Cup Race, the event was staged until 1906,
the Tourist Trophy races being established in the Isle of Man the following year.
Of interest are the regulations covering the machines entered for these early races. The motorcycles
were not permitted to weigh more than 110 lbs, exclusive of petrol, oil, spare parts and accumulator where coil ignition
was fitted. If sparks were provided by a magneto, an extra 3 kilos could be claimed.
The competition was open to teams of three riders each, plus a reserve, representing their respective country.
Great Britain did not fare at all well in any of the three years
of the pre Isle of Man series, perhaps as a result of remaining forever straight in contrast
with the Continental stars who never resisted a chance to ignore the rules when a suitable opportunity presented itself.
In this section are shown some of the great characters who rode in these International Cup Races.

19   So rich an atmosphere one might be forgiven for believing the
subjects in the scene are actors of the early French film industry. Seated
on a Griffon machine is rider Lamberjack being briefed by possibly the
Marquis de Mouzilly St Mars, sporting gent if ever in road racing matte
of the time. In this 1904 event, Lamberjack took third position in t
final placings

20 [*Left*] Near Dourdan, 11th September 1904, and Marcel Bucquet on another Griffon machine prepares for the 'off' in the eliminating trials held some three weeks prior to the official Cup Race.

Note with interest Bucquet's Griffon, which has suitably braced but unsprung forks and the very high gear that he is pulling [size of engine pulley] for what is obviously a single gear transmission system. In the process of lightening the machine, the rear wheel belt rim is generously drilled

21 [*Middle left*] Yet another and indeed snappy looking Griffon with 1904 winner Demester effecting a classic pose. No question of exhaust pipes, be it seen!

22 [*Middle right*]   And in the Italian camp, Guippone, seen here standing behind his twin cylinder Peugeot. The leather case on the front fork assembly còntains the battery for the machine's coil ignition system

23 [*Below left*]   British track racing expert, Rignold, alas, lowly placed in the International Cup Race. The racer is a Lagonda, fitted with one of the very earliest JAP engines

24 [*Below right*] Raising a dust in this action study, the briefest of French captions to this mystery rider might read … Thomas 'au virage'. Observe both young and old enjoying the spectacle

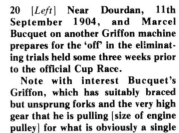

FOR KING & COUNTRY

Then Jack Service, DR, maybe three stripes proud and doing his patriotic bit for Victory Day. Antique matter now of the mind, recalling the regular advertisements appearing usually on the front page of *The Motor Cycle* and *Motorcycling* during the World War Two years.

Consider, if you will, an earlier period of our twentieth century time, however, sometime about 1910 when the architects of war might be persuaded that the motorcycle in the dawn of any future conflict would serve a vital role. Confirmed by 1914, thousands of civilian motorcyclists volunteered for military service to ensure the lines of communication could be held on any front.

If an unsophisticated setting, such is the peculiar excitement of reality, a reality perhaps of Flanders mud and hard worked machines as heavy horse at plough. Come the oft times sweating and begoggled riders, many with spare driving belts across their bodies in bandolier fashion. Their despatches delivered, might have saved the day.......*they light a well earned cigarette and pass their ordered way.*

25   Be prepared for the clever Dicks who fancy that advertising material nowadays is bound to appeal if included is an 'old car' or an 'old motorcycle'. More than often do they suggest that 'multi' indicated more than a single cylinder engine for the Rudge. However, we surely know it was the variable gear, providing many ratios, that supplied the tag!

26   Calling all youth, calling all youth - July 1940. Members of the Eltham MCC who were classified as being in 'reserved occupations', gave much of their spare time to training young motorcyclists to help win the war. In times of earlier conflict, even the anti-motorcycle brigade had realised the advantages of the motorcycle with its ability to provide a speedy and economical vehicle for communications. All too quickly has this been conveniently forgotten, when a period of adversity is past.

Encouraged by *Motor Cycling*'s editor Graham Walker with his never to be forgotten weekly Dispatch Rider register coupon for completion, hundreds of young motorcyclists between the ages of 18 and 20 'enlisted'. The various motorcycle clubs undertook to provide the basic training prior to the lads receiving their call-up papers, and eventual service as military motorcyclists.

'Aviating in the picture is a true piece of solid stuff mounted on a 348cc KTS model Velocette. Remarkable days.'

27   The 'Jimmie James' in service dress, 1943. The War Department were quick to appreciate the rapid mobility of troops, particularly paratroops, provided by the economical lightweight motorcycle. Really quite a humble little two stroke, the James built at Greet, Birmingham, was fitted with a Villiers 9D 125cc engine/gear unit. This is the 125 ML [Military Lightweight] model. Simplicity in the electrics department, with both ignition and lighting coils situated in the flywheel - in other words....no motor running, no lights. Note the pressed steel front forks, semi bolted up frame assembly, and masked headlamp. The paratrooper is wearing what was called 'battle order', in which the minimum amount of kit was carried in the small pack, while the knife would have been used to 'quieten' the occasional enemy sentry at a very strategic moment

28   Five months before the outbreak of war in 1939 and the army of today's all right. The sporting season was just getting underway again for the Ilkley and District Motor Club when Yorkshire's first important motorcycle trial of the year, the Ilkley Grand National, was held over a moorland course which started and finished at Chevin Top, near Otley. Out of a good entry, by '39 standards at least, of 45, including most of the leading riders of the county, the army was represented by the 49th West Riding Divisional Signals.

The Triumph mounted rider, wearing one of the original one-piece type of Barbour suits over uniform, looks as though he may have been saying something not too complimentary to the cameraman. Meanwhile, Arthur makes to effect a bit of competition card attention to our squaddy's back

LADIES A'WHEEL

Never an all male preserve, motorcycles and motorcycling have attracted the lady enthusiast over many years.
Most times remaining entirely feminine in such a pursuit, notable exceptions to this order have been recorded by
eye witnesses observing full-bodied creatures as Wotang's daughters astride
the heavy metal, challenging time and the elements in Wagnerian stamp.
In the sporting field, elderly citizens may well recall a beautiful Muriel Hind as Trials winner supreme
on Rex machines in a pre Kaiser War setting. Of the 1920s,
Fay Taylour and Dot Cowley, sirens of the Northern dirt tracks, on their screaming Scotts.
Perhaps a whiff of this feminine enthusiasm might be captured in a short address given by a dear old thing
at an Association of Pioneer Motorcyclists luncheon in London
some ten years ago. The marvellous soul spoke of her forthcoming marriage to Reggy in 1911,
'marred' by a nocturnal romp on brother Harry's eight valve Indian.....'I was so captivated by the experience
that, alas, my fiancé remained just that for another three years....I fear his mother never quite forgave me.'

29 [*Above*] Lady motorcyclists at Brooklands in July 1920 with **Miss Rita Don**, sister of the well-known Kaye Don, seated on her Zenith, with Coventry Victor engine. Mrs H S Powell, nearest camera, has settled for the rare lightweight Metro Tyler machine with Birmingham-made Metro engine and two stroke power unit.

One usually associates Zenith motorcycles with thumping great vee twin JAP engines, although the horizontally opposed twin versions, as shown here, existed in fairly large numbers. A novel feature of all belt-driven Zeniths was the famous Gradua gear, brainchild of the Zenith Company's chief designer, the late Freddie Barnes. A variable gear was available, by the operation of a coffee grinder handle, situated by the rider's left knee. Turning one way or another would either open or close the inner faces of the crankshaft mounted belt pulley, according to the road condition presented. At the same time, correct belt tension would be maintained as the rear wheel moved in special slots at the fork ends of the frame

30 The lady motorcyclist of 1912, gentle dignified, and yet - one may be sure understood more than a little of the culinary art and general housekeeping. A period when we could rightly boast of stability within the country, alas, long, long past!

With a dainty booted foot placed on the footboard of a 1911 Scott [air cooled barrel and water cooled cylinder head], our feminine subject shows to advantage the Mackintosh motorcycling costume of the pre-Kaiser War years. Incidentally, the appendage beneath that footboard is a foot operated warning bell, a feature to be found on many original veteran Scott machines.

A traditional feature of all early Scotts was the open-frame design making it an ideal machine for the skirted lady rider

31 [*Above*] Some idea of the refreshing informality of motorcycling competition in the early 1920's can be appreciated from this charming scene of Mrs Baxter engaged in 'conflict' against the clock.

It is the Harrogate and District MCC's Hill Climb and while a comfortable looking observer stands his post, our lady motorcyclist pilots her two-stroke Baby Triumph with obvious pleasure

32 [*Left*] A rather faded but indeed unique photograph. Taken in 1909, it shows Mrs Eric Myers, wife of one of the directors of the original Scott Company at Bradford. At a period when the Scott motorbicycle was just going into general production, certain proprietary fitments were made and supplied by the brothers Ben and Willy Jowett of motorcar fame. It is said that the machine's originator, Alfred Scott, was undecided as to whether cylinder barrels and heads should be water cooled during these formative years, and Mrs Myers' model has only water cooling of the heads, the barrels being air cooled in natural manner. In advance of many of its contemporaries, the Scott was fitted with a kick starter mechanism, the lever being situated at the rear fork end. When the lever was depressed by the rider, a length of rod, terminating in several links of light cycle chain, actuated a ratchet faced drum, which engaged with the two speed gear on a quick thread device, thus turning the motor over. A powerful scroll spring would then throw the starter mechanism out of engagement after use

33 [*Above*] **Mention the name Marjorie Cottle to any long distance Trials addict of pre-war days and thoughts are immediately conjured up of quite a remarkable lady, who could handle a motorcycle with all the skill and dash of any man.** Serving a novitiate in the simpler One Day Trials of the early twenties, Miss Cottle was later offered works rides on Raleigh machines, including the 1923 'Six Days'. Perhaps one of her most memorable performances was a single handed attack on the coastal perimeter of England, Scotland and Wales, in which she covered nearly three and a half thousand miles in 11½ days during 1924. Favouring overhead valve BSAs in the early thirties, Marjorie rode in several International Six Days Trials, and is here seen checking in at Donington Park in September 1933 where the specified speed trials then took place. Miss Cottle was the only lady competitor to finish the tough ordeal in that year.

The gentleman in the check cap and goggles looks suspiciously like George Brough, being the only type to wear a cap in such a special way

34 [*Left*] **This charming picture prompts me to enquire of two things: where have all the lady motorcyclists gone today, and why is there less dignity about the game nowadays, when we are told that this is the time of affluence?** Gathered around, prior to the start of the Weller Cup Pillion Trial in June 1932, our ladies make a splendid casual pose for the cameraman.

Long before quite ridiculous men would foster the equally ridiculous safety neurosis, providing that the bike was taxed and insured one could go out and ride in his pyjamas if he so wished. One felt decidedly free.

So much the period, those lightweight fur trimmed goggles [1/6] from Halfords, or the Hutchinson waders, magnificent things. I have only to close my eyes and concentrate, and I see it all again, as if it were yesterday.

Typical feature of Panther motorcycles, more so in pre-war days, was the no down-tube frame, clearly evident here

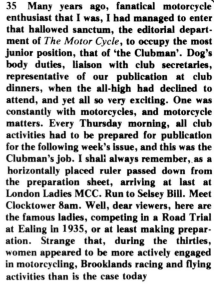

35 Many years ago, fanatical motorcycle enthusiast that I was, I had managed to enter that hallowed sanctum, the editorial department of *The Motor Cycle*, to occupy the most junior position, that of 'the Clubman'. Dog's body duties, liaison with club secretaries, representative of our publication at club dinners, when the all-high had declined to attend, and yet all so very exciting. One was constantly with motorcycles, and motorcycle matters. Every Thursday morning, all club activities had to be prepared for publication for the following week's issue, and this was the Clubman's job. I shall always remember, as a horizontally placed ruler passed down from the preparation sheet, arriving at last at London Ladies MCC. Run to Selsey Bill. Meet Clocktower 8am. Well, dear viewers, here are the famous ladies, competing in a Road Trial at Ealing in 1935, or at least making preparation. Strange that, during the thirties, women appeared to be more actively engaged in motorcycling, Brooklands racing and flying activities than is the case today

36 Glamour in the 1950's - take note of that, any spoilt trendy of the 70's! Just about 50 miles down from London at the famous Kursaal, Southend-on-Sea, 20-year-old Maureen Swift was riding the Wall of Death in 1953. No newcomer to this thrilling spectator sport, Miss Swift had been 'doing the boards' since she was sixteen, even to sitting side saddle at 40 mph, as we see her here.

Discovered by ace rider Tornado Smith, Maureen took to the job after only three weeks of instruction, which prompted Smith to say that she was the quickest learner he had ever known.

Whether Wall of Death riders still favour the American vee twin Indian machines, I know not, but my memories must be only of these slightly jazzy motorcycles, highly painted and distinctly 'audible', which went so well with the dashing circus type scene. I feel sure that there must exist a place for them in the Sir John Betjeman heart!

37 During the period that I have been associated with motorcycles and motorcycling, I have become aware of the great enthusiasm for the game increasing in strength if one turns both attention and journey to the North of England. Perhaps it is a case of a healthy respect for machinery of all types in industrial areas of the country, and where a phoney sophistication that places the motorcar as a veritable god is not so tragically obvious.

The motorcycle is accepted as a legitimate means of transport and has its own very special place in traffic systems.

Here we see a storm-coated lady rider competing in a North Manchester Club's 'Rough Riding Afternoon' during January 1933

TT Machines & Aces

No greater test of man and machine in the science of rapid tempo has yet been found away from the Isle of Man
course. Of the TT motorcycle, much a specialised device, tuned to a predetermined pitch
by the professional in his line of business and worked to run
all out in any gear as and when required. If true to the letter of the distant Tourist Trophy rules
should the machine have remained much as any Arthur's workaday steed,
yet all the dash and glamour of the series never more held in the highest appreciation
than when a truly international flavour of works teams
on out and out Grand Prix motorcycles came and raced their way in the 1930s, 40s, 50s and early 1960s.
Then the TT rider, idolised by any real enthusiast as a veritable god.
Of interesting ingredient as his agile brain, rapid reflex, body fitness and courage in generous proportion.....
a very special fellow.

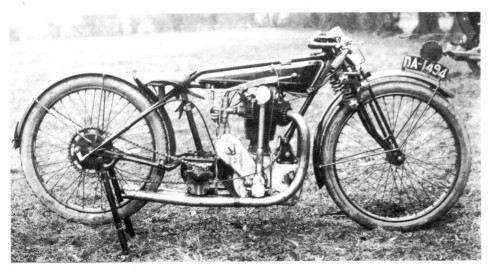

39 Possibly one of the first appearances of
the overhead camshaft Sunbeam. A rare bird
indeed. During 1925 experiments were
conducted, with a model incorporating a more
advanced system of valve operation as
opposed to the then accepted pushrod engine,
the result being a 'cammy' Sunbeam. Pictured
is the prototype, still retaining normal coil
valve springs, at a Speed Trial meeting in
which the legendary George Dance was the
jockey. In the Senior and Sidecar TT races in
the Isle of Man, hairpin valve springs were
used for the first time on a racing motorcycle
with the introduction of the new 'Beam'
although its performance was far from
impressive. After 1925, the whole design was
shelved, a reversion was made to push rod
engines and nothing more was heard of the
overhead camshaft Sunbeam. Perhaps the
designing team should have persevered, for
Velocettes, by 1926, had won the Junior TT
race, with their own overhead camshaft model.

38 [*Above*] One is inclined to say over and over again in one's mind, racing motorcyclist.. racing motorcyclist....for somehow this speed shot of Charlie Dodson, neatly tucked in on his works 250 New Imperial, during the course of the 1934 Lightweight TT, typifies a period in motorcycling history where everything had become all 'just right'. Perhaps we might call it sophistication without vulgarity. On another page in this album reference is made to the mighty vee twin from New Imperials, equally as seductive as the quarter litre jobs, but never as successful in racing competition as the smaller machine. For all the splendid CJPD style, Charlie was later to retire, giving the Rudge marque a one, two, three victory

40 [*Left*] The Isle of Man 1914 and Senior TT winner for that year, Cyril Pullin, is shown seated on his Rudge Multi. Of great interest is a workshop notebook maintained by Pullin which gave excellent detail of his machine as follows: Like the other Multis, the big single [85x88mm - 499cc] had a Ruthardt magneto, Senspray carburettor and John Bull belt for the twenty speed gear. It differed from standard in having a higher compression ratio [4:1], a 5% nickel steel inlet valve with a shrouded neck. Cams were ground to give an inlet opening at 5° BTDC, closing at 37° after BDC. The exhaust opened at 47° before BDC and closed 20° after. Flywheels were polished and loaded in the rim to balance 45% of the reciprocating mass. A lightened connecting rod carried needle roller big end bearings, but a plain little end bush. The cast iron piston was carefully lightened, and two 1/8ins piston rings fitted. Piston clearance was made almost double that recommended by contemporary engineers.....and this proved advantageous. 3000 rpm and 80 mph [on the level] could be obtained. So much for progress, say I!

41 'Battle Irons at rest'. The marvellous
conglomeration of narrow section tyres on
spindly wheel rims, flat tanks and solid frames
of TT machines, Douglas Promenade 1923.

We may imagine that the shot was taken
either before or just after a spot of practice
over the near 40 mile Isle of Man course.
Nearest the camera is a Cotton fitted with a
Blackburne engine, while facing it [No 48] is
the very first of the overhead valve Nortons,
the marque so soon to become synonymous
with classic 'Island' victories.

Our Manx cyclist as he concludes his
mobile tour of inspection has just passed the
famous 600cc Norton/Hughes sidecar outfit
'Willy Stikkit', facing to the left. With
Tommy Mahon as passenger, Graham
Walker certainly 'stukkit' to secure second
place behind the Freddie Dixon piloted
Douglas outfit in the sidecar race. George
Tucker on yet another Norton took third
position at 52.07 mph

42 Possibly one of the trickiest corners of the entire 37¾ mile TT Course.....Governor's Bridge. Our picture shows semi-works Raleigh rider Arthur Tyler coming a 'box of tacks' at just that point, during the 1930 Senior TT. Now much a forgotten make, Raleigh motorcycles were made as early as 1899 by the famous cycle manufacturers at Nottingham, but it was not until 1922 that the first racing model appeared in the Isle of Man, with a single entry in the Junior TT of that year. Not greatly encouraged by the Raleigh's retirement in the race, the marque did not appear again for the TT series until 1928, with a '7th' in the Junior and '8th' in the Senior. By 1930 the Senior models were reputed to be capable of 100 mph and indeed with one winning the 500cc class of the Austrian Grand Prix. After 1933 motorcycle production ceased completely, to be replaced by manufacture of a three wheeler, called the Safety Seven, with its single front wheel. Discontinued after 1937, the three wheeler gave way to a policy of pedal cycle production only

Drawing reproduced by courtesy of "Motor Cycling"

LIGHTWEIGHT
TOURIST
TROPHY
RACE
(Promoted and Organised by the A.C.U.)
WEDNESDAY JUNE 8
1932

42A Referred to from time to time by the seasoned TT fan ... clutched as near sacred matter by the motorcycle crazy youngster's first time in the Island, the TT programme. Possibly not entirely unconnected with the Depression years austerity, the quality of both paper and photographs was not good, but who cared, when the races were on and going well

42B The most challenging road racing course in the world

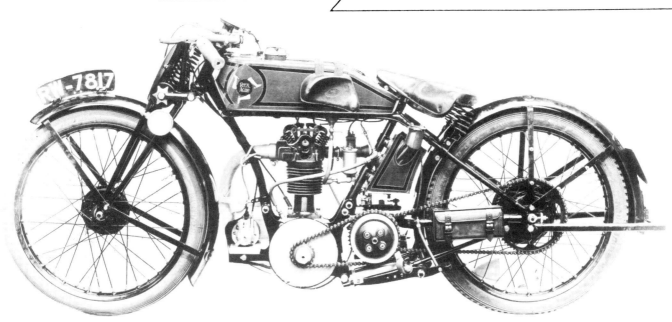

43 A racing Rex Acme Blackburne *circa* 1929. One of the true sporting motorcycles of a Golden Era. 'In' at the very dawn of the British motorcycle industry, the marque, prior to 1919, was known purely as the Rex, but later could not only boast of possessing the additional Acme, but also the Manx coat of arms, indicating that a sound schooling in the Isle of Man races had been achieved. Typical of the early racing Blackburne engines was the outside flywheel which was known literally to 'ring' at certain speeds. Interesting points to note on this TT model are the additional set of chain stays, fitted to prevent the frame whipping, plus the little heel pedal rearward of the footrest, which permitted the rider, during the course of a long race, to pump an extra shot of oil to the engine. Racing had now become such a desperate business that it was more than a rider would dare to do to remove a hand from the handlebars to operate the former plunger type assembly on the tank top. Perhaps the greatest Rex Acme star of all time was the late Wal Handley, a very courageous rider

44 Anyone who has participated in motorcycle road racing will know exactly what was passing through Jimmy Guthrie's mind, as the seconds tick away prior to his departure into the cut and thrust of the 1933 Junior TT. Idolised by thousands of fans during the in-between-war years, this truly remarkable Scotsman from Hawick, although riding various marques until 1930, remained loyal to Nortons as a works rider from 1931 until his unfortunate death in the German Grand Prix some six years later. Tough, fearless and possessing a deep intelligence, Jimmy typified the schoolboy hero racing motorcyclist with such fine qualities. Indeed his number of TT wins and Continental Grand Prix firsts are too numerous to detail here. Dedicated to his profession, Guthrie would maintain complete physical fitness during the off season, when he would ride his own TT Replica Norton to an Edinburgh gymnasium for weekly weight lifting exercises. Debatable, but I think that Jimmy Guthrie must be rated as one of the greatest riders ever known to the sport

45 As a member of the *Motor Cycle* staff
reported in his copy when covering the Senior
TT race in 1932....'Graham Walker knows
Signpost Corner so well that he can find time
to smile at the camera as he passes through'.

To anyone over 40, the name Graham
Walker is synonymous with motorcycling in
all of its exhilarating spheres. Former Norton
teamster and works manager, a spell at the
old Sunbeam works, and then Rudge to the
end of his racing career. From 1938 until the
early fifties, Walker occupied the editorial
seat of the publication *Motorcycling* and so
genuinely acted the father figure for all
motorcyclists. Suffering a left leg injury about
the time of the First World War, it was
necessary that an adaptation had to be made
to the rear brake control in order that Graham
could correctly operate it. This will explain
why there exists in this photograph the rather
strange attachment about the left foot rest.
How we miss Graham, and those brilliant TT
commentaries of his. We oldies must be
pardoned for saying that things will never be
the same again!

46 Later to become no mean performer in
the sophisticated world of motor racing,
Charlie Dodson is no doubt reflecting on how
fast his lap times would have been in practice
for the 1933 Lightweight TT, had it not been
for a flat rear tyre. Happily no misfortunes
were encountered by CJPD during the actual
race, however, with a well ridden second place
finish behind Syd Gleave [Excelsior].

Winner of both the 1928 and 1929 Senior
TTs, on Sunbeam machines, Dodson possessed a very characteristic method of riding
in which he employed a special body lean
technique, totally different from other
contemporary styles of cornering a racing
motorcycle at speed.

Although of considerably slight stature, his
rivals were left in little doubt as to his great
physical strength

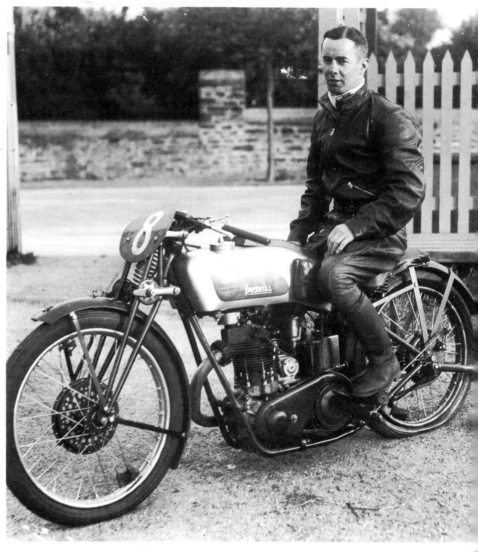

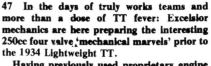

47 In the days of truly works teams and more than a dose of TT fever: Excelsior mechanics are here preparing the interesting 250cc four valve 'mechanical marvels' prior to the 1934 Lightweight TT.

Having previously used proprietary engine units, mostly JAPs, for their competition machines, Excelsiors had produced their own novel H J Hatch designed 'four valvers' for the 1933 TT series with a win for one of their riders, Syd Gleave, at 71.59 mph. Two camshafts, one in front and one behind the cylinder and mounted in the crankcase, operated a single push rod to each set of valves, two inlet and two exhaust. Not entirely uncomplicated, the rockers [four] actioned the radially positioned valves by a system of a small piston that slid in a bush in the rocker housing, motioned in turn by the push rod. The rocker heels stood side by side on the piston head. Somewhat difficult to maintain and keep in a good state of tune, Excelsiors in 1935 turned their attention to a less complicated system of valve operation, when the two valve overhead camshaft 'Manxman' was introduced

48 Considered by most racing enthusiasts of mature years to be the prettiest racing 350 ever, the Velocette achieved this final accolade with the introduction of the KTT model Mk VIII in 1939. Pioneered way back in 1936, the special Oleomatic rear suspension system had been fitted solely to works machines, but was now at last available to the private owner. The actual geometry of the suspension layout was not unduly complex, although the air sprung, oil damped units had to be very carefully maintained for, if a speck of dirt or a leaky valve decided to offend, the suspension would promptly collapse. Just visible at the top of New Zealand rider L V Perry's suspension unit [right] can be seen the capped valve, which of course would have to be connected to a normal tyre pump from time to time over a season's racing. With a compression ratio of 10.9:1 and running on a 50/50 petrol benzole mixture, the beautiful Mk VIII was capable of about 110 mph. In the forefront of this picture is Australian rider Frank Mussett, who finished tenth in the '39 Junior TT on the machine shown

49 Such a businesslike creation with meaty motor and crying 'go' from every angle of appreciation, no wonder it was claimed by many to be a potential 'world beater' as far as motorcycle racing was concerned; the 492cc vee twin New Imperial, born in 1934, never quite achieved that enviable position in classic competition. Raced both in the Isle of Man and at Brooklands, mostly in the hands of S 'Ginger' Wood, it gave more than adequately a high speed maximum in attempting track records. Not possessing the best of steering characteristics, it failed to provide formidable opposition to other makes in road combat, however, although any enthusiast lining the Bray Hill section of the TT Course could be assured of fireworks as Wood attempted to hold it on a sober line. Virtually a scaled up version of New Imperial's considerably more successful single cylinder 250 racer, it did in fact make several appearances at Donington in slightly revised form during the immediate pre-war years. In 1949 its positively final showing was at the Hutchinson 100 meeting at Silverstone when it came under starter's orders with rider Tony Norris in the saddle

50 [*Above*] An Isle of Man postman takes a brief moment of relaxation to watch German DKW works rider Arthur Geiss scream his forced induction 250cc two stroke to seventh place in the 1935 Lightweight TT. Although this was the first year in which such remarkable machines had come to the Island they were by no means new to the road racing scene, and were much a force to be reckoned with in Continental events, indeed since the early twenties.

Possibly the noisiest racing motorcycles ever to appear in classic road racing, and combined with their shimmering silver finish, they could be classed as the motorcycle that was different.....1930's Exotica!

The 250cc DKWs were what is referred to as split single two strokes with an additional pumping cylinder placed on the forward end of the crankcase, its piston being of the double acting type. Two carburettors were situated on the pumping cylinder's special head. Note the neat little radiator for the water cooling system!

Upward gear changes were made in combination with an ignition cut-out system, giving sharp explosions and lengthy sheets of flame from the DKW's megaphone exhausts

51 [*Left*] A plus-foured Tommy Hatch is relaxed mood during the 1933 Senior T] pre-race activities. The story of Hatch's entr; for that year's Isle of Man race is interesting indeed not without complication. For all thei charm and a solid backing from hundreds o devotees, the Scott had become a non competitive device in big time racing afte 1930. With plans to revive the Sidecar TT i 1933, it was decided that two Scott outfit should be built, one by the Yorkshire paren company and the other by the Liverpoo agent, A E Reynolds. Pilots would be the grea Scott ace Harry Langman and Tommy Hatcl respectively. All very exciting, althoug pressure of other business prevented eithe outfit being completed, and the race itself wa cancelled owing to a lack of sufficient entrie Determined that a Scott should be repre sented in the Island, Reynolds utilised certai completed parts of the abandoned sideca machines to provide Hatch with a solo mode for the Senior event. Although reluctant t ride it, as he considered it no match for th four stroke opposition, Tommy finished i fifteenth place on this Scott Reynolds Specia the occasion being his last road race of all tim

52 More than worthy of being included in the title 'Continental Menace', the Italian Moto-Guzzi will always be remembered in the history of classic competition. Built near the shores of Lake Como, the Guzzi designers worked on the principle of strictly functional machines, minus any frills, with strong emphasis on light weight. The horizontally positioned cylinder was most times a traditional feature of 250 Moto-Guzzi engine layout although there was the mighty 120° vee twin 500 racer, fashioned in 1933. A 1934 TT version is here shown with more or less conventional frame design, although later versions were fitted with a novel system of rear suspension, in which the spring boxes were situated beneath the engine/gearbox assembly. Hardly visible in our picture is the outside flywheel on the nearside of the Guzzi's overhead camshaft motor which revolved in a clockwise direction, the motor running 'backwards'. The idea to mount the oil tank partially inside the fuel tank was a simple method at cooling the lubricant

53 *Chacun à son goût*, but to my mind the racing motorcycle of the nineteen thirties represented near perfection, if not mechanically then at least aesthetically. Short frames, meaty looking motors, diminutive racing saddles, and often the wrap around oil tank, as it was then referred to. Standing behind a classic example of my particular joy, namely the 1934 TT Husqvarna from Sweden are, at extreme left, Ernie Nott, while far right is the one and only Stanley Woods, both riders having been signed up to race the 350cc and 500cc vee twins for the 1934 season. Although reputed to be very fleet devices, both Nott and Woods retired during the Senior TT of that year, the Junior race providing Nott with a third place, however. Developed into an even more appetising piece of raceware during the late thirties, the Husqvarna was to enjoy certain Grand Prix wins, and many fastest laps on the Continent in the hands of works rider Ragnar Sunnqvist. Centre gentlemen in this IOM picture are G Kairn of Husqvarna and mechanic Holt

54 As I proudly wrote in my book of the Norton, 'they raced from victory to victory, with almost monotonous regularity'. In its own way as much a British institution as roast beef, the Norton was, perhaps still is, a name synonymous with solidarity and winning form.

This 1933 post Senior TT shot presents an impressive line-up of men and machines, not forgetting the Boy Scouts who, to this day, continue to serve so well in scoreboard duties particularly. Retaining the classic bore and stroke dimensions of 79x100mm until 1936, the 490cc Senior Nortons of '33 now had cylinder heads of bi-metal construction in which a bronze skull was surrounded by an aluminium-silicone shell. Previously, save for a spot of experimentation in marrying two different metals during 1932, the Nortons possessed all iron engines. Additionally, in line with modern practice, the machines shown employed aluminium cylinder barrels with a cast iron liner.

Brains behind Norton technical advance were Arthur Carroll, re-designer of the overhead camshaft power unit in 1930 [on Woods' left] and development engineer Joe Craig [on Woods' right]. Waving the flag, and why not?

55 Sans gimmicks, sans coloured leathers, sans vulgarity, even sans cissies. Possibly the most famous plot of ground to all United Kingdom motorcycle road racers and followers of the sport alike, being the start/finish area for the TT races, the Glencrutchery Road, Douglas, Isle of Man.

Approaching the moment of coming under starter's orders are competitors for the 1936 Lightweight [250cc] TT. A great character of racing, C W 'Paddy' Johnston, stands aside his Cotton [2], while M Simo from Spain [4] looks away from his Terrot machine to concentrate on the four valve Rudge to his left. Behind Johnston's Cotton can just be seen part of the then new overhead camshaft four valve works Excelsior machine, which was ridden into second place in this event by H G Tyrell-Smith. The winner rode New Imperial Number 12 in our picture, being Bob Foster, only two days into his honeymoon at the time. Elsewhere in this album are two pictures of Foster's bike, in captivity after the war

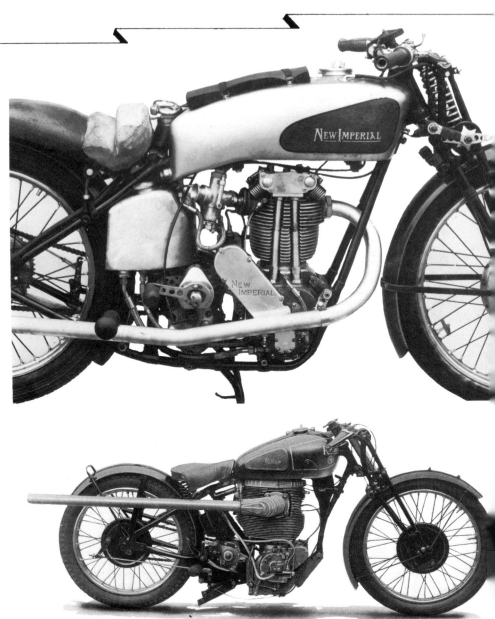

56 A picture too good to miss out, even though I must admit to including more than a fair share of the New Imperial marque. To my mind one of the most aesthetically pleasing of pre-war British racing motorcycles, the New Imp looked right, and therefore assumed, was right. Shown here is the official works racing 250, one of three in fact that were built for the 1935 season. Design and construction of the push rod operated overhead valve power units followed fairly conventional lines, although great emphasis was placed on the most ideal system of engine lubrication. From 1931 onwards down draught carburettors and pistol grip fuel tanks became the order, with only detail changes on the factory racers being made through the years up to 1936 when the company 'retired' from any further fast competition work. Excitingly typical of all the sophisticated stuff around the 'golden thirties' was the hummock seat pad, forerunner of the 'slide back and down to it' items of later years

57 This 1935 500cc rotary valve Rudge Cross TT model typifies the 'different' designs that made their appearance in pre-war races. Conceived by R C Cross of Bath, several versions were built for road or competition use, including a very sophisticated twin cylinder two stroke of 250cc. Perhaps the four stroke TT model was the most famous of all, however. Retaining the basic features of the Rudge frame and crankcase, the huge Cross engine was indeed unique. The rotary valve consisted of a cylindrical unit situated across the top of the cylinder which had ports connected with the inlet and exhaust systems. The valve which rotated at half the engine speed was chain driven from the drive side of the machine. Pre race gossip in the motor cycling press of '35 stated that the cylinder head valve and valve bush were water cooled, with five pints of water being contained in a finned housing surrounding the assembly. Later, a correction was made, advising readers that, in fact, the coolant was oil. With a compression ratio of 12:1, the Rudge Cross surprisingly ran on No 3 Commercial petrol and maximum power delivered at 6000 rpm.

Ridden by A R Brewin in the Senior TT of 1935, the Rudge Cross lay in 23rd position on the first lap in a time of 33m 24s at a speed of 67.8 mph, compared with Jimmy Guthrie's Norton performance of 84.23 mph. Came lap two and Brewin was out with what was described as 'plug trouble', although later it was learned that the alloy rotary valve housing had more or less disintegrated. The interesting concept did not appear again in any 'Island' races

58 Indeed a remarkable occasion for that great Italian ace Omobono Tenni, being the first foreign rider to have won a TT race, and on a foreign machine. A sunny summer's day in June 1937 with a well satisfied Tenni taking a drink after completing 264¼ miles of racing at an average speed of 74.42 mph on his 250cc Moto-Guzzi to take the Lightweight Trophy. An interesting period as far as 250cc racing is under review, for in the previous year to Tenni's victory Bob Foster had won the Isle of Man race on a New Imperial which was to be the last time that a British machine - and indeed a push rod operated overhead valve design - would win the Lightweight. Always in the running, the Birmingham made Excelsiors could never quite make a first place, at least in the later thirties, as the Continental marques Guzzi, DKW and Benelli, each in turn, made their determined challenge

59 The very spirit of the Manx Grand Prix 1938 style. Originally called the Amateur TT for genuine private owners as opposed to works machines ridden by professional riders, the races were, indeed still are, staged in the month of September in the Isle of Man. During the great years of motorcycle road racing, nearly all famous TT aces served their novitiate in 'The Manx', one being the famous Johnny Lockett, later to be an official Norton star. Johnny is seen here, however, in a typical sports jacket of the thirties, preparing his own Norton during his Manx 'school' days. The model is classic, no ridiculous advertisements for dog meat or washing up liquid adorning its noble being. New for the private owner in 1938 was the Norton plunger rear suspension system, although the famous 'Roadholder' telescopic front forks were to remain solely for the official factory bikes until 1947. Just visible is the Edgar Franks designed conical front wheel hub, which strengthened considerably the whole assembly and provided better heat dissipation for that hard worked area of a racing motorcycle. A parting remark: at one time everything was all so different....need I say more?

60 The term 'full flight' is most appropriate to describe Stanley Woods' posture as he storms down Bray Hill on his Senior Velocette in the 1937 TT. It may not be appreciated other than by those who would claim to be either Velocette 'knuts' or dedicated followers of motorcycle racing that the Hall Green Company had produced 500cc Velos for their strictly works riders only as far back as 1934. These early models were, in fact, based very much on the already distinguished overhead camshaft 350s. By 1936, however, the 'big' Velocette really chimed into the racing scene as far as Stanley Woods was concerned, providing this quite remarkable rider with a second place in that year's Senior TT, to be repeated exactly in the two following years. Very much a Velocette feature on all works racing models from 1936, and 'private owner' 350cc KTT jobs in 1939, the patented swinging arm rear suspension system, in which the units were air 'sprung', pioneered what is now accepted practice on nearly all motorcycles. Springs have, of course, replaced the oleomatic principle

61 I suppose if we were to collect just anything from a past period with a desire to make as new, we would be guilty of many things too numerous to mention. That I was to learn some years ago now that the one and only works 250 New Imperial on which Bob Foster had won the Lightweight TT in 1936 had been broken up was indeed very saddening. The machine was unique in many respects, for it had a gear driven clutch assembly in its unit construction motor, which necessitated the engine running backwards as it were. It was also the last time that a British racing motorcycle, and indeed push rod operated overhead valve power unit, was to win the Lightweight series of TT races. This beautiful little bike was capable of about 94 mph in 1936, which to many an old enthusiast could be described as a fair turn of speed. Just after the war, the very distinguished road racer Jock West raced the New Imp again in one or two meetings until at last it found its way into the hands of such lucky men as Mr Henthorn of Barnston, Cheshire, who is pictured here. By the battledress top that Mr Henthorn is wearing he may have been, at the time, on leave or just recently demobbed. Great days!

62 'If only I could get my hands on one of these' is the regular comment of any dedicated post-vintage racing enthusiast. The 1938 genuine works, no less, 250cc overhead camshaft Excelsior Manxman, BR BR category. Considered by the 'thirties connoisseur' to be the prettiest racing 250 ever, our picture shows *The Motor Cycle* staffman 'Paton' taking a spin on Ginger Wood's model, following its finishing second in the 1938 Lightweight TT.

The Coventry based Excelsior Company, originally trading under the name of Bayliss, Thomas and Company, in 1874, when high quality bicycles and fittings were manufactured, progressed to motorcycle production with both racing and utilitarian models in the programme. Until 1934 proprietary engines were fitted in most cases, when the Excelsior Company, now at Tyseley, commenced manufacture of their own engines in both overhead valve and overhead camshaft form. The actual racing, Manxman models followed quite conventional lines, although in 1933 and 1936 experiments had been carried out with special 4 valve racers. The more normal two valvers were, and indeed are, however, the enthusiast's delight

63 Ted Mellors, eleven years a TT rider, from 1928 to 1939. Associated with works Velocettes from 1936, Mellors was to become 350cc European champion some two years later. Although one of the great riders of the thirties, Ted won a TT race only once, which was the 1939 Lightweight, in which he rode an Italian Benelli. Our picture shows a rather rain soddened victor being congratulated by Signor Benelli at the conclusion of the race.

By 1939 the Benelli works had built an experimental four cylinder 250, but the single cylinder models were quite capable of matching the products of rival factories, where a course did not necessitate all-out speed as a premium. DKW from Germany enjoyed a system of forced induction, while the 1939 Moto-Guzzi single cylinder racers were fully supercharged. Beautifully designed and constructed, the unblown Benelli had a double overhead camshaft engine unit, the camshafts being driven by a train of gears, enclosed in an aluminium housing on the offside of the cylinder. In 1950 the famous little Italian Benelli rider, Dario Ambrosini, won the Lightweight TT on a machine very similar to Mellors' 1939 model and bagged a second place in the following year's event on a slightly updated job

64 As was the custom until as recently as the 1950s, members of the motorcycle press would take a ride on TT winning machines. Usual practice was to set out from the mountain section with a 'fast as we dare' whizz perhaps back to Douglas.

With Ted Mellors in this picture, Graham Walker prepares to set out with Mellors' machine to record his own impressions of the classic little racer in June 1939. Much was made of the light weight of the Benelli and there exist memories of GWW lifting the complete machine waist high while puffing splendidly at a cigarette.

Observe the ultra-rear footrests for high speed stuff and the spare valve spring secured to the front forks

65 A time when Great Britain not only ruled the waves but enjoyed more than a few Isle of Man TT victories. How sad it is that one must needs seek solace in the past!

A pleasant shot, taken in June 1938, only a few minutes after Harold Daniell had won the Senior race with that never to be forgotten last lap speed of just over 91 mph. Daniell's Norton, literally plastered with dead flies here, differed from previous works machines of the 1937 period, not only in frame and engine construction techniques, but perhaps more evident, the telescopic front fork assembly. Slow to accept the 1938 refinements Daniell had made it quite clear that he preferred the earlier and indeed lighter girder fork models, and no doubt would have ridden one, had he not been under Norton contract to race the newer machine. However, victory smiles, certainly conceal any doubts he may have had about the bike. Also enjoying the moment are Norton chief race mechanic, Bill Mewis, and technician Frank Sharratt on Daniell's left

66 The third occasion in 28 years of TT racing that a machine not of British manufacture was to win the Senior race. Refreshing themselves at the conclusion of the 1939 event are German Army Sergeant Georg Meier [left] the winner, and Britain's Jock West, who came second on a sister machine. While British manufacturers were still only toying with supercharging systems for racing motorcycles [private entrants at Brooklands excepted], Germany had virtually perfected forced induction techniques some time in 1936, particularly with BMWs, of which a later model is shown here. Of very neat design, the rotary blower faced forward in between the front down tubes, while a single carburettor was mounted in a slightly staggered position, just in front of the right hand cylinder. Naturally, the carburettor was connected to the supercharger, where tubes passed rearward to connect up with both cylinders' induction ports. Perhaps the motor was now too potent for the cycle parts, or was it the shaft drive, for indeed Meier's BMW showed more than a little tendency to snake viscously as he circulated the Isle of Man course thirty five years ago

66A Now nearly seventy years old, the silver Tourist Trophy still awarded to the winner of the Senior TT

67 The very spirit of racing on public roads!
Velocette riders G H Hayden and Y Gauchy
[France] round the Isle of Man's Governor's
Bridge during practice for the 1939 Junior TT
races. It is possible that some Velocette
fanatic will question whether both models are
KTT Mk VIIs, but I will risk suggesting that
the Velos are 1938 private owner jobs, as yet
still without the famous oleomatic rear
suspension. Some lucky lads did race the new
for 1939 rear sprung Mk VIII machines. The
works bikes had employed spring frames from
1936, however. What about the Mk VII? a
superb racing overhead camshaft 350, first
available to the competition rider during the
early part of 1938. Although solidly framed
and with cylinder head fins rounded off at the
corners, compared to the official works
Velocette 'springers' with their 'square' fins,
the Mk VII was not dissimilar to the pukka
stuff in many ways. With fine roadholding
characteristics, and a maximum speed of over
100 mph, one will understand why the models
were very much in demand. Exactly twenty
five were made before the even greater Mk
VIII superseded it

68 Perhaps the spirit of optimism existed in
both camps for not only was the Porcupine
AJS, as it later became known, plotted during
the very heat of World War II, but also new
and very advanced fully supercharged DKWs
were actually undergoing track tests in
Germany in 1941. Such things were bound to
raise the morale of Tommy and Fritz enthusiasts alike.
    Originally designed as a supercharged twin,
it became necessary to revamp the AJS when
the ultimate governing body of motorcycle
racing, the FIM, dictated the 'blowers' would
be out for a post-war programme of sport.
When at last the 'Porc' - so named because it
had a series of very finely shaped cooling fins
around the cam boxes - appeared in 1947 it
looked every bit the type of racing machine
one could call a winner. Its career up until
1954, however, in various states of modifi-
cation, never quite achieved the full glory
expected. The double overhead camshaft
power unit of 500cc had a 360° crankshaft,
which was geared directly to the gearbox, the
engine running anti-clockwise. These Ajays
that gave a beautiful drone from their mega-
phoned exhausts at least provided a 500cc
World Championship for Les Graham in 1949

69 [*Above*] Wise men of motorcycling had urged the British motorcycle industry to produce a supercharged racing multi cylinder machine now'. Velocette rallied, and had built the famous 'Roarer', too late, however. Norton stuck to the well tried and certainly proved unblown single, and certainly paid for it in the 1939 Senior TT races. The vee four supercharged AJS was not, in all honesty, reliable enough to be considered a 'cert'. The wise men's utterings had come in 1936 in time to halt the 'Continental Menace' as it became known. We were licked on our own stamping ground, the classic Isle of Man Course. Winner of the '39 Senior TT, Meier hurls his blown BMW around Hillberry and on to victory. Brief specification of Meier's machine was a horizontally opposed twin cylinder engine of 494cc, the supercharger positioned at the forward end of the crankcase, upon which was mounted a single Bing carburettor. The mixture was then forced through the pipes, one of which is shown passing beneath the nearside cylinder to the inlet ports.

Similar details of the BMW appear on plate 66

70[*Left*] One of very few road racers equally at home behind the keyboard of a typewriter or scorching down Bray Hill in the Isle of Man on one potent two-wheeled device or another was Fergus Anderson, alas, no longer with us to provide motorcycle journalism at its best. One of the original stars of the Continental Circus, being of a type that preferred the busy life of charging from one race meeting to another, mostly in Europe, 'Fairgooz', as his Italian Moto-Guzzi mechanics affectionately called him, achieved his greatest successes on Guzzi machines in the early post-war period, winning countless races for the Mandello based factory. This Isle of Man picture was taken in 1939 when Fergus rode a semi-works DKW of the double split-single two stroke system with charging pump. Anderson retired in the Junior race on this very noisy 350, but managed a 28th place in the Senior race on the same machine. Fortunately, the 'Deek' still exists and is entered from time to time in post-vintage races, although no spares are now available for this rather complicated and temperamental racer

71 [*Above*]   A sight to stir the blood of any British enthusiast, as genuine Norton racing bikes are prepared for the 1950 TT in temporary workshops in the Isle of Man. These Nortons were the very last word in racing single cylinder design and had the famous Featherbed frame which was, and still may well be, the finest roadholding layout existing for motorcycles. One may recall Graham Walker's commentary on the 1950 TT series, in which he described the new Nortons as being totally different from anything that had previously come from Bracebridge Street, the models to be ridden by Artie Bell, Johnny Lockett, Harold Daniell and a really bright young man from St Helens, Geoffrey Duke. Time passes so rapidly and we are obliged to ask ourselves, did this all happen twenty seven years ago? Golden times indeed

Note exhaust pipe extension in megaphone, fitted in order that these race machines could be tested on the roads 'out of race hours'

73 [*Above*] **Two great stars of Norton racing fortunes, A J [Artie] Bell [*left*] and Harold Daniell, with spectacles. Taken in 1949, the picture shows something of that unique, indeed exciting atmosphere, of riders turning out for practice over the 37¾ miles of the classic Isle of Man TT course.**

Bell, who first raced in the Tourist Trophy series in 1947, was a works entry from the very start for Norton Motors, and other than his retirement in that year's Junior race, he was never placed lower than fourth in a TT career that lasted until 1950. Senior member of the Norton works team, Harold Daniell had served a long apprenticeship, his racing years dating way back into the late twenties, and private owner performances on Nortons, with a brief excursion on AJS raceware giving him the Joe Craig invitation in 1938. Winner of three Senior TTs on works Nortons, the most notable being the '38 event, in which he had made that never to be forgotten 91 mph lap. Later both men rode the duplex framed Featherbed Nortons, Bell enjoying greater success with the new design

74 [*Below*] **Every picture tells a story, or does it? Smiles all round, except for 1947 Lightweight TT winner, Manliff Barrington [248cc Moto-Guzzi, Number 23]. Keen motorcycle road racing enthusiasts will hold that the race was Maurice Cann's, also Guzzi mounted [Number 3], and that something had certainly gone wrong with the timekeepers' watches.** Starting five minutes before Barrington, in the way of the special timed system for TT races, Cann was riding literally as the scalded cat, and had built up a fine lead on time, during the first lap, only to stop during the latter part of the race to fit a new valve spring. Such temporary retirement permitted Barrington to close up sufficiently on time to a degree that threatened the now mobile Cann once again. However, leaving not one atom of dust to settle, Cann crossed the line, appearing to have more than adequately pulled back his time deficit, and indeed was acclaimed the winner. When the timekeepers made their final calculations, as Barrington finished, astonished officials were to learn that victory must go to Barrington, although the matter is debatable, even to this day

72 [*Left*] **Even in the immediate post-war years of austerity, excitement ran high as the race enthusiast looked forward to a sport he had been denied for five weary years. A time of the one and sixpenny haircut, grey pin stripe flannels, hairy sports jackets, and so many coupons, and last but never least, the private owner Norton was again available to the racing man. Perhaps the times were reflected in the black wheel rims.**

Shown is the 1948 Manx model with double overhead camshaft motor, and that simply glorious slab sided tank with characteristic serrations at its bottom, to prevent the possibility of splitting. Pioneered during the late pre-war years, the famous Norton 'Roadholder', front forks were now fitted to all production race models, although the plunger rear suspension was standard on genuine racers after late 1937.

It was on this type of machine that one of the greatest road racers of all time, Geoff Duke, ascended the ladder of fame

75. First and second home in the Ultra Lightweight [125cc] TT of 1951. Belfast rider Cromie McCandless, the winner [62], congratulates team-mate Carlo Ubbiali [Italy], Number 71, in the winners' enclosure. Not given a very bright reception by the know-alls of motorcycle sport, 125cc racing was judged by them to be 'boys' stuff' of little interest, with even suggestions that many of the machines would have literally to be pushed up and over Snaefell Mountain on the demanding Island circuit. It is pleasing to recall that more than a few cynics were obliged to eat their felt hats, particularly when McCandless, Ubbiali and third place man Guido Leoni all finished the race at speeds in the 70s. The twin overhead camshaft F B Mondials were Italian machines and the first really serious four strokes to contest ultra lightweight competition in a post-war setting. At peak revs of about 9000, these pressed steel forked models with plunger rear suspension were capable of about 95 miles per hour

76 Claimed by the motorcycling intelligentsia to be the greatest racing motorcyclist Germany has ever produced, Werner Haas is shown here, well on his way to second place in the 1953 Ultra Lightweight [125cc] TT. Killed in a flying accident some two years later, the official works NSU team, of which Haas was their number one rider, were disbanded.

Sensational would be the only way to describe the NSU's re-emergence to the racing scene, against their doubtful performances in the nineteen thirties, with both supercharged and more conventional breathing devices. As if blessed with the magic touch, everything appeared just too good to be true, for the NSU in the early nineteen fifties, with both wins in all classic races for the single cylinder 125cc model, and the indecently fast 250cc twin.

No upstarts in the motorcycling world, the Neckarsulm factory were indeed true pioneers in the production of motorcycles, even to producing a novel two speed gear assembly as a proprietary fitting to many other machines in the early years of this century

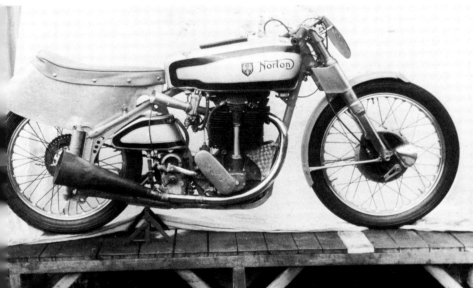

77 And there were special distinctive Nortons finished in a light green colour, meticulously fitted with all kinds of racing niceties. They were the work of Francis Beart and gained as much admiration as the pukka race Nortons from Bracebridge Street. This 350 model prepared in 1950 typifies a Beart Norton in all its special glory, with lowered frame, shaped fuel tank, immense cylinder finning, seat tail and copious drilling of certain sections. On the front forks, aluminium deflectors have been fitted to direct a good blast of air onto the exhaust valve area, while the fitment on the foremost end of the front mudguard was designed to prevent it becoming an air scoop when the machine was travelling at high speed. The Francis Beart crest was always in evidence on the tanks of these special Nortons.

Still active in racing motorcycle preparation Beart now concentrates his art on Italian Aermacchi machines

78 When British World Champion Eric Oliver, with his famous Norton Watsonian outfit, retired from top flight Grand Prix racing in 1954, the German sidecar crews with their immaculate BMWs, were naturals to take over the reign of power. Ideally suited to the special ingredients required in truly purposeful three wheeler racing, the BMW may only now be challenged by the remarkable Konig two stroke power units that are steadily gaining popularity. Cornering in a style 100% professional is shown World Champion and winner of so many sidecar races on British soil, as well as nearly every Continental circuit, German National Max Deubel, with Emil Horner in, or rather just out of, the sidecar. When the fashion for a kneeling position on all sidecar machines found favour with nearly every first rank 'pilot', Deubel remained one of the very few who preferred the more conventional attitude of sitting on his BMWs, and winning into the bargain. Our shot was taken in 1964, when Deubel had well and truly arrived, as the saying goes

BROOKLANDS

Brooklands - the very name is sacred to those that knew it in its heyday and, strangely, to those who could never be
of its thirty-two year period.
A marvellous place for the men and women who were actively engaged in its community life
and the terminus for our adventurous summer schoolboy's thirsty travel.
Brooklands, as the proving ground for most things designed to counter time, worked on in sometimes gloomy sheds
and put to test on rippled runs of concrete
linked by vast bankings, Members and Byfleet, in that order.
Brooklands, remembered on March days 1938, when all the greats would gather to try their latest competition ware.
The three lap outers or the mountain races, leathers, Castrol R
all about the place and the Meyrowitz man, who gave a pair of goggles to every type
who gained his Brooklands Gold Star on lapping the track at 100 mph.

9 [Left] Stanley Gill takes a puff at a more than adequate cigarette as he is pushed off on his Alecto two stroke, after eleven hours of Brooklands record breaking, 3rd August 1920. Virtually a standard production model of the time, with no pretence to anything of a sporting nature, the Alecto was a simple 350cc, with belt drive, and stirrup front brake. At least the marque could boast of being the first two stroke motorcycle to break long distance records on that hallowed saucer of concrete, a few miles down from Waterloo, however. Long forgotten in the mists of time, to many the name Alecto will be just a name, for by 1930 the marque had vanished from the motorcycle scene, as indeed did so many others, killed no doubt by the never to be forgotten slump

The actual Brooklands spot in our picture is the run from the Byfleet Banking, across the Fork to the Members' Banking. Later, the famous Vickers sheds would exist alongside the Fork area, which eventually became the starting point for all outer circuit races

81 [Above] Spirit of Brooklands, early 1930s fashion. A Norton rider, now off the Home Banking, sweeps onto the fast Railway Straight in an outer circuit event

80 [Above] A splendid scene of Brooklands work in July 1920 when the well-known South Kensington dealers, Ballard Motors Ltd, entered this Harley Davidson [standard magneto model] and light sidecar on a time challenging spree. After 2 hours the outfit had covered 106 miles, while 9 hours later 609 miles were completed, speeds varying from 53 to 50 mph as the run continued. Petrol consumption worked out at 50 mpg. In the saddle is shown J D Marvin, who incidentally only sported one leg, while relief pilot here, about to act as ballast, is J A Sullivan. Each man took a 2 hour spell on the machine.

Typical of Harley Davidson motorcycles, the famous bottom link forks are fitted and just visible, the single lever Schebler automatic carburettor.

Marvin was a partner in the Ballard business and obviously wished to practise what he no doubt intended to preach

82 Common practice by necessity rather than desire in ultra modern racing, one-design events staged at Brooklands in the 1920s were introduced to provide an interesting diversion. In this picture, an absolute benefit for riders of Zenith machines, all of which had to have side valve engines and bore size not exceeding 85mm. Different carburettors were being used by some entrants, however. Winner of this novel race was the brilliant track performer, Kaye Don, in a time of just over 4 minutes at a speed of 64½ mph. Leading here just after the start, however, is C G Mallons. The very freedom of the place is perhaps expressed by W J Kelly [17], typical of a type who preferred to race bareheaded, and as far as is known, remained not the worse for it. He finished in ninth position

83 The interesting 350cc Chater-Lea of 1925 in Brooklands trim. One mostly associates the marque with that speed wizard Dougal Marchant, although certain complexities might well be cleared here and now as to the actual engines he used for his record attempts. It is usually understood that *all* Marchant's power units were the novel face cam motors, as shown in our photograph. Not so, however, for experimental adaptations were made to push rod operated overhead valve Blackburne engines, with fully enclosed camshaft, and its attendant drive. It was not until the mid-twenties, however, that the genuine face cam units were used, a system where the vertical drive was topped by a lobed disc on its uppermost end. The exhaust and inlet valve rockers were positioned at right angles to the disc, and fell into the natural grooves on the disc, being activated when either lobe raised the heel of the rockers. A novel design, indeed, although it is a matter of conjecture whether the whole project was ever worth the effort, for there is no indication that there existed any advantage over more conventional valve operating systems

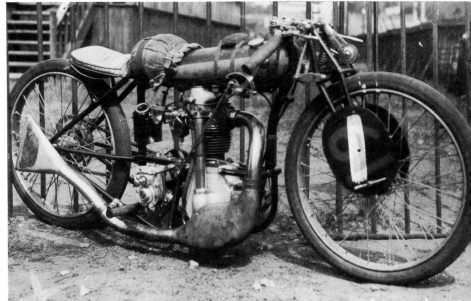

84 Another fine shot taken during the progress of the Zenith Scratch Race with riders hard down to it on the famous banking. Note shirt sleeve order for Number 5. Interesting were the prizes awarded for this novelty event where the winner received a silver cup valued at ten guineas, presented by Zenith Motors Limited. The runner-up was given the Zenith Gold Medal, plus three pounds, while third man home had another gold medal and one pound. Quite a dignified haul for 1920.

Elsewhere in this book, the Zenith motorcycle is described in some detail, a highly sporting device in its way yet favoured by many a country parson in the comfortable shires of a once prosperous Britain

85 [Above] And even a smile from dear old Norton as a jubilant group of enthusiasts make their way back to the Brooklands paddock or bar in March 1922. The good looking little fellow carried high is Rex Judd, after having raised the world's flying kilometre record [500cc class] to nearly 90 mph. James Norton wheels in the machine that looks as any sporting Norton of the period, but were we wafted back to this pleasant occasion we should find that we were looking at one of the very first overhead valve jobs. The push rod design maintained the classic bore and stroke measurements [79x100] of the side valve models at 490cc. A remarkable designer and engineer was James Landsdowne Norton, for he had already schemed the ohv power unit as early as 1913 and had spoken of desmodromic valve operation and speeds of 160 mph as distinct possibilities decades before such things were manifested. How the whole pattern of British motorcycle racing prestige may have been influenced we can only hazard a wishful thought, for Norton the brilliant passed away at the early age of 56 in 1925

86 [Left] A time when reference to Big Twin could only mean a delectable thing with vee cylinder formation, while the word 'rorty' could never be far away in any appreciation. At this period, George Brough's masterpieces were still mainly fitted with side valve JAP engines, although the faster SS 100 with overhead valve arrangement was at least off the assembly jig and ready to go. Later to be adopted on all the big Brough Superiors other than a few special models, the famous Castle bottom link front fork inspired by the success of such fitments on Harley Davidson machines. This model sports forks of slightly more conventional design, however.

Note the finned valve caps atop the cylinder heads, spoken of as fir cones by the passing admirer and indeed those in the game

87 [*Above*] Nearly all eyes on Fernihough, Christian name Eric ... 'Ferni' to his friends and admirers. What finer location than the finishing straight area at Brooklands, taken here in reverse direction for starting purposes only, then down to the start for outer circuit stuff.

The magnificent Brough Superior is shown in its 1938 form with supercharger added, working with Bowden carburettors on the draw and puff principle. The occasion: a test run for the Brough during an interval in a British Motorcycle Racing Club meeting. Sad indeed that a few months after this photograph was taken, Ferni lay dying alongside the mangled Brough when attempting the World Speed Record on the Gyon Road, Budapest.

Sleek laddie in sports jacket, assisting in the pushing job is John Rowlands, intimate friend of Fernihough, while figure second from right in the picture looks suspiciously like C E Allen now President of the Vintage Motorcycle Club

88 [*Right*] Agreed, the New Imperial marque has enjoyed more than its quota of prints in this *OLD MOTOR* album, but most pictures of these machines are just too good to leave out, and I must therefore remain unrepentant in including yet another. Based on the fairly humble 150cc unit construction job of 1932, which served the young motorcyclist so well, H R Nash decided to reduce the capacity of one of these models to 123cc in order to attack certain records at Brooklands in 1934 and '35. Appreciating that the little push rod operated overhead valve machine had limitations regarding all out performance, in the custom of many Brooklands racing mounts some very neat streamlining was fitted around vital parts of the New Imperial. We see here Mr Nash setting off successfully to break the standing mile and standing kilo records on 16th October 1934. A year later the same rider on the same machine took the world's flying kilometre record at 70.01 mph

89 I make no apologies for including this 'real' picture that has appeared so many times in various motorcycle publications and books. My reason is a simple one, for the presentation exudes that very special atmosphere of Brooklands goings on during the late thirties. The occasion was the completion of the World's Three Hour record [350cc class] in 1938. Certainly, no straightforward run without incident, the special 7 gallon fuel tank fitted to permit as few pit stops as possible had split at the seams and forced an abandonment of the original record attempt. 'Never say die' being the motto of ace Brooklands tuner and racer Francis Beart [extreme right], the Norton was wheeled out once more with a standard 4 gallon tank as shown to attack the 'Three Hours' again. Rider H A R Earle seated, although quite a track and road racer, did not appear to maintain the highest speeds necessary on this special Norton, which required Noel Pope, standing next to Earle, when taking over during the course of the run, to work at full stops to regain lost time. The sporting group also includes John Rowland, well-known Brooklands habitué

90 A whizz down the Railway Straight at Brooklands sometime around 1938. In the saddle, Motor Cycling's editor Graham Walker, enjoying himself with the Rudge machine on which he had won the Senior Ulster Grand Prix ten years earlier. The occasion was all part of a feature that appeared in Motor Cycling, in which the very latest Ulster model Rudge was matched against the earlier device regarding performance, handling, etc. Not entirely surprising was the revelation that both machines returned a maximum speed in the mid nineties, although it was reported that general roadholding characteristics of the newer model were much improved. Progress in its right perspective!

It never ceases to amaze me that so many power units of racing motorcycles of the twenties and early thirties, with their totally exposed valve gear, proved to be both efficient and reliable. In the case of the racing Rudges, for example, only the very crudest of systems maintained any form of lubrication to the operating department of the valves, although the engines were turning over at a maximum of 5200 rpm, giving an all-out speed of 100 miles per hour

91 A feature of nearly all motorcycle racing at Brooklands in its sophisticated years was the unique system of handicap starting. The slower men were sent on their way first, to be followed by the mid range riders when starter's flag was dropped again. Finally, the death or glory boys were despatched at 'scratch' position; sometimes more than a minute behind the 'limit' men. A maximum of two pushers were permitted to send riders on their way. Several well-known Brooklands characters are shown hovering around entries 2, 3 and 4 in this 1939 shot of the start of a 'mountain' race. On the extreme left is Maidenhead rider Ron Harris, while appearing in a somewhat reflective mood sits Johnny Lockett on another Norton, with the famous Francis Beart in riding coat and cap, standing rearward of the machine. L J [Les] Archer, complete with most of the male members of his family, waits patiently aboard Velocette [4]. Any Brooklands regulars will not require me to suggest who the scratch men were!

ONE FOR THE RECORD

**Dear old Professor Joad once defined time as a measure between one set of events
and another, direction being optional.
The Modern English Dictionary serves to state that 'against time' is a striving to do something in record time
or the shortest time possible, with the utmost speed.
For some strange reason, Man has felt compelled to challenge the stuff that waits for no one, be it in thought,
athletic or vehicular competition. When successful, he may enjoy a certain satisfaction
and he is lauded for his efforts.
Perhaps the greatest medium of modern times provided for the challenger
in his fight 'against the clock' is the mechanically propelled vehicle. Some have chosen to use a motorcycle
with sometimes a sidecar attached. Many have perished in their attempts,
while those spared from such a sacrifice contain an insatiable thirst to improve upon the 'last' record.**

92 [*Above*] Vienna, June 1932 stop Australian Alan Bruce on 996
supercharged Brough Superior wrests world's max sidecar speed record
from Germany's Ernst Henne stop Record taken on Tat Road stop Flying
kilo 124.40 mph stop Flying mile 123.15 stop Congratulations stop

94A Now Captain Eyston was a motor car man, although the advertisement appeared in *The Motor Cycle* for 1938. More important, however, there is that special pre-war atmosphere about it, so it must be included at all costs

93 A meeting of the mighty on the Frankfurt Autobahn in 1937, when Winkler, in white linen suit and streamlined helmet, contributed to the establishing of nine world and six international class records on, of course, a DKW two stroke. The model was a specially prepared 175cc job for Winkler's series of 'runs', and featured, as is clearly seen, a cowling around the steering head, and faired forks of aerodynamic section. Discs were fitted to the rear wheel. To obtain the very purpose of ultimate speed, Winkler adopted a near prone position on the DKW, his feet placed on special footrests about the rear wheel spindle. It is interesting to note that a hand change system was used for operation of the gears in preference to the more usual foot control. Centre figure in the group is Bernd Rosemeyer, DKW ace, as well as brilliant driver of the Auto Union racing cars. It was in one of the special record devices that he lost his life on a later occasion

94 Swedish Records Week at Ostersund [North Sweden] 5th - 11th March 1930. The rider on the remarkable little Husqvarna is F Mannerstedt, who broke Swedish Records Class B/S flying kilometre and flying mile on ice, no less. Typical of record machines forty or more years ago, the forks are bound with insulating tape, which was then lacquered, all of which provided a better form of streamlining. Untypical is the kneeling position adopted by Mannerstedt, but strictly functional, however. In order to lower the machine as much as possible, a 16ins diameter rear wheel was fitted. Supporting both machine and rider is the famous German Rekord Meister, Ernst Henne, who successfully retained the 'world's fastest' title on BMW machines for many years prior to World War II. In this picture Henne is wearing a white rubber suit, no doubt to give him a modicum of comfort from the icy conditions

95 On to the 250cc class of record breakers at Frankfurt, with Ewald Kluge seated casually aboard a basically DKW model ULD road racer that had undergone certain wind cheating refinements in preparation. Undoubtedly the very last word in racing quarter litre two strokes at this time, the ULD was designed during the Autumn of 1936, proved itself in international races in 1937, giving Kluge the title of European Champion 250cc in 1938. The water cooled power unit was of split single design, in which a common combustion chamber served two separate cylinders, while forward, just beneath Kluge's left foot, was a vertical charging pump with a rotary valve on top. To this was attached two carburettors, one on either side of the machine. The rear suspension layout was a combination of plunger and swinging arm systems where the spring housings were originally bolted to the frame ends as shown here in 1937. Later models of the ULD had the housings brazed to the frame, when it was found that the former design had given a too whippy rear end under racing conditions

96 Those little items of motorcycle magic that had us feverishly thumbing through the pages of *The Motor Cycle* and *Motor Cycling* on Thursday mornings in the 1950s. We could rely on Norton or AJS - often Velocette - to bring something out of the bag to 'keep us in front'.

As was the custom at the conclusion of the racing season, British motorcycle manufacturers took their specially prepared machines to Montlhéry track near Paris to spin off the year with a new set of world motorcycle speed records. Norton as usual were well to the fore in 1953 with a 500cc model lowered sufficiently to permit a rider to adopt a kneeling position 'inside' the aluminium streamlining. With this device the late Ray Amm was one of three riders to take 50 kilometre and 50 mile, 100 kilometre and 100 mile world all-class records 'in the hour'

Warming up the 'Silver Fish' is Norton mechanic Charlie Edwards, while to the left stands the works wizard Joe Craig. Ex-bomber pilot and renowned sidecar racer Eric Oliver gets set to take over the controls

97 A picture taken just before the war, outside the offices of the Triumph Engineering Company at Coventry. All the activity is centred around the start of an exhausting test of both the Speed Twin model [*left*] and the Tiger 100, under ACU observation. The two machines were picked at random from dealer's stock and then subjected to a strenuous riveting of over 1900 miles on British roads for a period of 6½ days, at an average speed of just over 42 mph. On completion of the road tests, in which the Triumph models had battled through severe snow storms in the Glen Ogle area of Scotland the machines were ridden directly to Brooklands, where they put in six hours of continuous high speed lappery. On their return to Coventry, both motors were stripped to reveal that the pistons had picked up slightly during the complete ordeal, although basically the units were in excellent order. This will give some idea of the moral obligation that manufacturers possessed in pre-war days to the needs of their potential clients

98 John O'Groats to Lands End or vice versa, even the double distance has been the challenge before so many motorcyclists since the very earliest days of the game. Here two Wolverhampton enthusiasts, E T Turvey and J J Davenport, are being congratulated by AA Patrolman Jackson after their 903 mile journey in September 1950. Time taken for the non-stop run was exactly 23 hours. The Royal Enfield machine is a typical example of a proper unsophisticated motorcycle of the early post-war period, with no pretence to the crazy fairground 'sports' models of today. I remember these Enfields so well, just simple push rod operated overhead valve 350s, with all the performance one ever really required, and comfortable to ride. For some peculiar reason, current fashion demands that we should sit a bike as a monkey on a stick, and long gone is the comment of any true enthusiast who would refer to 'a nice riding style'

CONTINENTAL CAPERS

Motorcycling in the Continental way has always been an attraction for me, and for a variety of reasons.
Premier thought in this direction is an appreciation of a certain well-balanced sophistication
and maturity in the use of a motorcycle. The device is accepted as an alternative means
of transportation to the motor car and thus enjoys its own very special place
in the system of things. It is not assumed to be the poor rleation of the car.
Secondly, and for ever a fascination, is the Continental motorcycle
as a structure. It possesses features that indicate sound and functional engineering thought
in its design and the total absence of crude clip-on fitments that have kept other manufacturers in other lands
wallowing in the pedal cycle period of more than fifty years ago.
Then there is that special smoothness, nearly impossible to describe with the written word.
in styling that borders not far from aerodynamic principles, and all as much of the 1930's as it is today.

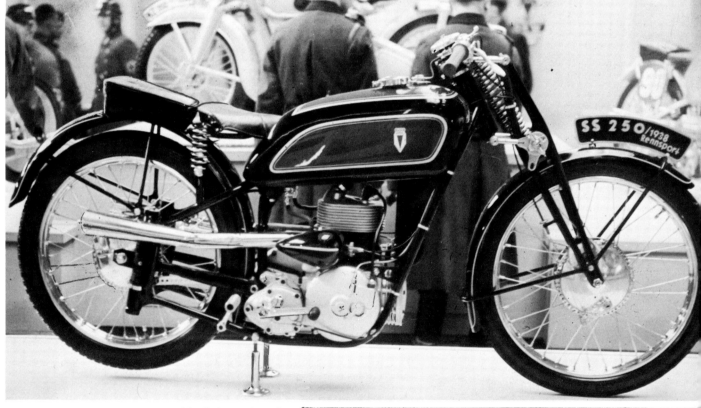

99 [*Above*] Humble by comparison with all the exotic works DKWs of the late 1930s and yet a speedy little racing 250. From about 1934 onwards it was possible for the private owner road racer in Germany to purchase what has become known in recent years as a production racing motorcycle. The SS 250 Rennsport DKW seen here at the Berlin Show in 1938, which had now shaped into quite a sophisticated model from previous years' designs, was not built in the DKW racing shops but on the normal assembly line with standard road models. Certain features of the SS followed pukka works practice, although rotary valves were never fitted. The forward facing charging pump housing can just be seen between the front down tubes, while shields protect the side mounted carburettor, one on each side of the cylinder block. Not being quite such thirsty beasts as the works bikes, the fuel tank was not of such immense proportions on the SS model. Notice the neat radiator for the water cooling just beneath the tank nose. Just prior to the war, two SS DKWs came to England, purchased by Noel Mavro-gordato and speedway ace Frank Varey. Mavro rode his at Donington, Varey in the '38 MGP

101 [*Above*] Avus in simplicity! Some years to go before brilliant white stone statues of dead heroes, concrete surfaced track and that quite indescribable grandeur of all that was German prestige racing of the 1930s. Here in 1925 we see the start of the German Motorcycle Club Championships with a BMW rider nearest camera, while Norton and Triumph marques are much in evidence. Note the hot cross bun type of racing helmet worn by many of the riders!

102 [*Right*] An imposing view of part of the Avus track, Berlin 1935. Typical of many Continental racing programmes, both motorcycles and cars compete in their separate events on the one day. I use the present tense as it is still very much the system, although not entirely appreciated by the motorcyclists should oil droppings and rubber dust be deposited by the four wheelers during practice periods.

At one time considered to be the greatest ultra high speed course in Europe, the Avus consisted of linking up two lengthy sections of Autobahn, with very steep banking at both ends. A perfect course for the pre-war supercharged BMW and NSU racing motorcycles, where sheer flat-out speed rather than perfect roadholding qualities was of greater importance. Perhaps the Avus will be remembered mostly for the fantastic duels between Mercedes and Auto-Union Grand Prix cars on hot summer Sunday afternoons during the late thirties

100 [*Left*] There is a tendency for many an enthusiast to refer loosely to all DKWs being supercharged, although this not entirely correct. Until 1939 there existed only models that employed systems of forced induction by gear or crankshaft driven charging pumps. It was not, however, until the last remaining months of peace in '39 that the fabulous - if I may employ such a trendy word - US fully blown models in 250, 350 and 500 forms were born. At last a supercharger in the strictest sense, being Cozette-Zoller type and chain driven, was mounted horizontally, forward of the crankcase, above which came the connected carburettors. Both the 250 and 350 versions were four piston twins, while the 500 sported three cylinders and six pistons. Although never raced in pre-war years, the US models appeared in the Isle of Man and were used in practice only, the same situation existing at the German Grand Prix in August 1939. Although fantastically fast, the 250 alone being capable of nearly 130 mph, non-supercharged versions were used in the actual races, being at that time more a known quantity. Pictured here is the 350 version of the US model

Walfried Winkler

103 [*Left*] That celebrated authority on the racing DKWs of the thirties, Erwin Tragatsch will say 'any big Continental race meeting in pre-war times without a two-stroke four-stroke battle was unthinkable'. So right indeed when one recalls those glorious, noisy 'Deeks', often so very much more fleet than other stuff, but sensitive enough to bring about their own destruction on some occasions. This classic German postcard of 1938 provides a beautiful 'shot' of DKW's senior rider, Walfried Winkler, heeled over in but one of literally hundreds of races in which he rode since 1925.

The DKW works still exist at Chemnitz, although now known as MZ[East Germany], where 'two strokes only' is still very much the order of things for competition and utilitarian models alike. Many of the original DKW staff still work with complete dedication there to honour the new MZ banner

105 [*Right*] Now Old Jones will most emphatically declare that this photo was taken during the post-war period, for he says that the type face on the Roll of Honour is far too modern for 1939. However, I have a feeling that it is just pre-war.

To the right, dear viewers, is the fantastic, forced induction, 250cc two stroke, water cooled DKW model ULD, ridden to so many Grand Prix victories by number one works jockey, Ewald Kluge, in pre-war days. One of two carburettors fitted can be seen mounted on the gear driven rotary valve housing. Number 12 is a Model RSS production racer, which any private owner could buy, and differed from the works machines in certain details, most important of which was the simpler system of forced induction that employed a pumping cylinder, the head of which can be seen at the bottom of the two front down tubes. Noisy and spectacular would be the best words to describe the racing DKWs in their heyday. All so much part of the Zschopau set-up of prestige racing in Adolf Hitler's Germany

104 [*Left*]The 250cc model US DKW makes a post-war appearance in West German national racing some time around 1949 Walfried Winkler, now perhaps a little thinner on top, is caught examining the clutch assembly prior to the start of battle.

It was Winkler who put in some very hard work developing the ultra fast US in the late forties and early fifties, only to be thwarted, if that may be considered the correct word when supercharged motorcycles were banned even at national meetings. It is known that this DKW of DKWs is alive and well presently resting somewhere on the Continent

For those that care to know, confuse not the ultra rapid three cylinder DKWs of the mid 1950s with any product from the Zschopau factory. Such machines were built in Ingolstadt in the Federal Republic of Germany and were of considerably different design although in some cases ridden by German pilots of the pre-war 'Dekkavay' school

106 It is only in recent years that the Japanese have surpassed the Continental manufacturers in two stroke technology, and then, in all fairness, may it be said that they have merely advanced already known principles and facts of the two-cycle engine. In 1932, the well-known Austrian Puch concern had produced a novel 500cc 'square four' unit, based on their 250cc 'double single' design. Differing from the conventional utilitarian 'pop pops' that we British riders used in our youth, Puch employed a system of twin pistons, a forked connecting rod and a common combustion chamber, the result of which provided considerably better transfer and exhausting sequences, and virtual freedom from four stroking. Not content with producing a much advanced two stroke, the sharp brains of the Puch designers at Graz decided literally to double up the number of working internals and cylinders to create this unique 'four'. Another ingenious feature was a servo operated clutch in the rear wheel of the machine

DESIGNS-Sometimes Classic, Sometimes Strictly Functional

It is not incorrect to suggest that the motorcycle may be a thing of certain beauty although appreciation, as ever, must be in the eye of the beholder. Man A will be excited by all the frills about it while Man B may express great delight in a functional design with each and every fitment tailored to serve the device as a whole.
The latter category of fellow will be, no doubt, of a more generous nature in that with his appreciation he shows a respect for the machine's designer possessing thus a brain for both the ingenious and economical type of construction. Seldom has there existed an occasion in the long history of the motorcycle industry when frill as opposed to classic has come together with the functional in equal and tasteful proportion on the one motorcycle.
One might consider some notable exceptions here and there, however,
At least for any admirer schooled in the way of things prior to the 1960's
there was always an ethical boundary where both camps could enjoy some common ground.
Sadly the products and indeed their promotion from some quarters
presently leave much to be desired. Morality in the exercise is given little or no consideration.

108 & 109 An exception rather than the rule during the competition years of the nineteen twenties .... the racing two stroke. One must applaud the efforts made by manufacturers to contest such serious events as the TT, with power units that were known to be inferior in performance to contemporary four strokes. Whether the producers of the Ivy considered that their 343cc two stroke stood more than a fair chance of a Junior TT victory is unknown to me, but in line with then factory policy 1920], the TT jobs were virtually next year's standard road models. At least the racing Ivys were known for their reliability and this alone was a fine selling point to yesterday's enthusiast. Brimming over with exterior controls of one kind or another, the Ivy possessed two brake pedals working two separate blocks on the dummy belt rimmed rear wheel, and another pedal that permitted the oil pump to be operated by a foot lever just beneath the carburettor bell mouth]. More typical of the period is the Sturmey Archer gearbox with its very familiar hand cum foot control, bolted to the seat pillar tube [shown right]

107 [Left] Gone the oil impregnated cobbled floor, gone the spats, and yet the Fair Isle pullover. Far away, the warm simplicity of it all. A rough guess would date this Model 18 Norton as about 1926, for it is fitted with Webb forks during the period when Druid pattern items were discontinued, and before forks of Norton manufacture were standard equipment. Our young man has possibly experienced some carburettor trouble, or perhaps he is just conducting routine maintenance. Quite incredible is the fact that the totally exposed valve gear worked so efficiently for other than a spot of oil from time to time, squirted onto those vital parts by the rider when he felt so inclined, no mechanical lubrication was employed. Note the breather leading from the crankcase to the primary chain case, and the Lissen mica sparking plug

110 Production line-up of ABC machines at the original works near Brooklands track in 1921. Designed, it is said, on Armistice Night 1918, by the remarkable engineer Granville Bradshaw, the ABC was indeed very much ahead of its time, incorporating very many features that to today's motorcyclists may be described as distinctly modern.

Sophistication and dignity would be the best words to sum up the layout of Bradshaw's masterpeice, with its horizontally opposed flat twin engine of nearly 400cc, even if the overhead valve gear required redesign, after

ertain structural weaknesses had been discovered a short time after roduction commenced. Leaf spring suspension was employed both front nd rear, the latter being one of the earliest examples of the pivot fork stem, now universally adopted by all motorcycle manufacturers. Quickly

detachable wheels, both fitted with hub brakes, were very much 'QD' as divided spindles were used. Ahead of other contemporary motorcycles, the ABC could boast of full electric lighting. Stink lamps would have been very old fashioned. It is said that the BMW was based on Bradshaw's design

111 A neat little sporting DOT of 1922. This simple design was introduced in 1921, following the failure of special TT 350s which featured such advanced things as ball bearing rockers and ball and socket tappet rods on the overhead valve vee twin motors.

Interesting points to note about this JAP engined side valve 350 is the position of the sparking plug rearward of the cylinder head, and the large bronze valve caps.

Producing approximately 8bhp a very similar model to the one shown finished seventh in the Junior TT.

So much the system of frame design at this period, the chain stays [unbraced] were a weak feature with a tendency for fracturing to occur where they joined the gearbox lug section

112 For all of its brilliance, the four valve 500cc Triumph Ricardo model was known to have taken many a good friend to higher duties when the forks had snapped at speed. Was there some weakness in the design around the steering head?

The 'Riccy' Triumph, as it was affectionately called, the engine being hatched by the late Sir Harry Ricardo in 1921, was to enjoy nearly five years of production before simpler two valve units replaced it.

For the Ricey, a steel cylinder barrel spigoted into a cast iron head and secured by five studs onto a metal to metal ground joint. Four valves, two inlet and two exhaust, placed at 90° between the pairs, and a very advanced feature, a slipper piston. Over the years of manufacture, certain modifications were made, such as angled exhaust ports in place of the original parallel ones, and dry sump lubrication replaced the total loss system. As a road racing machine, the Ricardo Triumph enjoyed moderate success, but fared well at Brooklands and at record attempts both in this country and abroad. This road job had an internal expanding front brake, Dunlop Cord tyres, Lucas Magdyno lighting set, lamps and bulb horn, circa 1924. An interesting motorcycle, pioneering the quartet of valves arrangement respected in the minds of present day designers

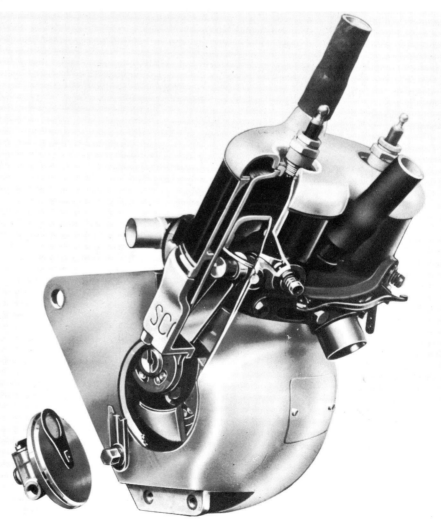

113 During my years of willing toil alongside one of the greatest freelance Scott engineers, a workshop motto was often repeated when things became more than a little complicated.....'The basis of all good engineering is simplicity'. My mentor had at one time worked in close liaison with Alfred Scott, and could be said to have known a thing or two, for he held that there was nothing quite like the twin two stroke water cooled Scott, for qualities of good function and simplicity. Pictured is a sectioned power unit of a 1925 Scott Super Squirrel, showing the overhung crank assembly, and the drive for the Best and Lloyd oil pump [situated on the nearside crankcase door]. On the early models the exhaust gases from both cylinders passed through a single outlet stub, while the power of the engine could be quickly reduced if required by operation of the half compression valves, just above this outlet. On either side of the centrally placed flywheel was riveted a sprocket which was connected up by chains to a 'high and low drum' of the two speed gear. The angled stub at the rear of the cylinders was the intake upon which the carburettor was mounted

114 A wealth of truth in the saying 'nothing new under the sun' for a scooter craze existed immediately after the First World War in much the same way as in the early 1950s. Not exactly a subtle difference, however, was that the Kingsbury scooter, as shown here, was based more on the child's model, at least cycle part wise. Rearward of the well shielded small two stroke engine the rider was expected to stand, it being assumed that the Kingsbury would only be used for short distance travel, such as shopping, letter posting, and so on. The tubular frame, on which is fitted the famous Tan Sad seat, would appear to have been fitted by this Kingsbury's owner, at a later date. If two persons were to be carried, the rider would assume the normal standing posture, while his passenger sat side-saddle. Divorced of his charge, the rider would then, no doubt, welcome the comfort of that seat! Interesting additional features are the simple form of front plunger suspension and the handlebar stem that could be folded down if necessary

115 A friendly policeman pushes a Scott rider off the course during the Lands End Trial in 1925. There is nothing particularly sensational about this shot, but the subject is warm and pleasing. Look at our motorcyclist, for example, dressed in riding breeches, tall stockings and brogues. No ridiculous goldfish bowl of a thing called a safety helmet, but the quite adequate leather flying helmet, which permitted long distance riding without a heavy head. Perhaps just as important was the fact that such dress did not bar one from a good hotel, and I speak with some experience on that score.

The Scott is one of the first of the two speed Super models, possibly the most famous road model from Shipley ever produced. Inside the pockets of many of the spectators we can be sure there exists many a rubber tobacco pouch and silver mount pipes. Why, why, why have standards declined in recent years, to bring nothing but sheer vulgarity?

116 Qualifying more for the TT section of this book, yet deserving of mention here as something built on a very functional line, vitally so for its original purpose. Linked in a very special way must be the names H R Davies and Jock Porter, both men having won TT races on machines of their own manufacture. Shown is Porter rounding Governor's Bridge on his way to a third place in the Ultra-Lightweight event on his 175cc New Gerrard in 1925. In the previous year's race, Porter had won on virtually an identical mount.

The rules required that these lightweight machines must not exceed 150lbs and close study of the New Gerrard will reveal the copious amount of drilling necessary to keep within that limit. Note the spindly ohv Blackburne engine with customary outside flywheel. Porter built New Gerrards for general consumption until the mid 1920s when production was taken over by the Campion Cycle Company in Nottingham. Manufacture continued until 1940, coincidental with Porter's retirement from the motorcycle scene entirely

117 Four cylinder 'superbikes' must not necessarily be identified only with the trendy days of the 1970s, for Ariels at Selly Oak, Birmingham, had produced the Edward Turner designed famous 'Square Four' way back in the early thirties.

Originally intended as a light 500cc machine, subsequent variations of the model were produced in 600 and 1000cc forms. Pictured is a 1935 600 four, with chain driven overhead camshaft, and forward facing carburettor. The two crankshafts were coupled together, in a very ingenious way and providing good attention was paid to maintenance in this department, no trouble would be experienced. Worn couplings were felt in no uncertain way, however, particularly on a trailing throttle, when one was descending a steep hill. Continued right up until the 1950s, the Squariel, as it affectionately came to be known by all enthusiasts, reached its peak of a certain popularity in push rod operated 1000cc form with, of course, foot change gear operation.

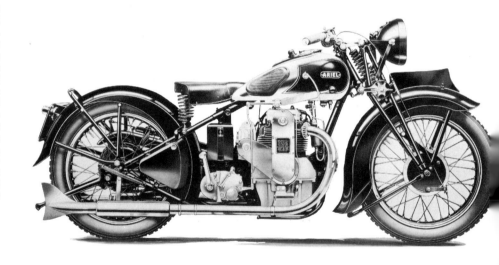

118 1935 and first appearance of the Vincent HRD, now fitted with an overhead valve engine, designed and constructed at Stevenage. Prior to '35, most Vincent HRDs were powered by the potent JAP engines and perhaps surprising to younger enthusiasts, also a Villiers 250cc water cooled two stroke in one of the utilitarian jobs.

The new Vincent designed engines were of the high camshaft type, which allowed short push rods to be fitted, which in turn reduced side thrusts on the rockers and valves. An unusual feature was the fitting of double valve guides, in which the rockers were forked and worked on special collars situated on the section of valve stem in between the two guides. The system used, incidentally, right up until the demise of the company in the 1950s. The bespectacled gentleman in this picture is the brilliant design engineer Phil Irving, whose brains were very much behind the fashioning of the new models. Here, with Jock Forbes, he is organising the new Vincent HRDs prior to a testing spin in the Isle of Man. Registration plate order

"CRUISER E39" TAX 22/6

During the Season 1934 the "Cruiser" has further increased in popularity. The advantages offered by this advanced design are more and more understood. It is realised that the "Cruiser" is not only the "cleanest" machine to ride—it is definitely one of the most comfortable.

The alterations for 1935 are confined to minor details only. The design has proved itself to be "right"—no necessity for alteration in its basic principles has been discovered. The "Cruiser" remains the best example of a clean and quiet motor cycle. Shields and rear mudguard are detachable, without tools. Cleaning is but the matter of a few minutes. A cruising speed

of 45 m.p.h. can be maintained over long distances. This model offers luxury riding at a very moderate cost.

249 c.c. Villiers Long Stroke Engine. Miller 6 volt Dynamo Lighting Set, with Ammeter and Dimmer Switch. Miller Coil Ignition. Four-speed Gearbox.
26" x 3·25" Dunlop Tyres. Electric Horn and Legshields.
With Petroil Lubrication

£36·10·0
£36 0 0

Code Word : "Cruisauto."
Code Word Petroil Lubrication : "Cruispetro."

General Specification on page ?

119 Looking back on my motorcycling days of youth, I perhaps unkindly gazed upon the Fanny Barnett 'Cruiser' as totally 'out', if one considered oneself to be an enthusiast. More was it the case of civil servants and doddering old fools just slipping over to the golf links on the 'enclosed', so very unsporting product from Francis and Barnett of Coventry. Now perhaps a more seasoned individual, I can appreciate the Cruiser for what it was, a quiet, hard working motorcycle that could be ridden in any weather, without any special clothing being required. It was indeed a much cleaner machine than most contemporary models of the thirties, and designed for a very specific purpose in mind, and its exhaust note could best be described as a muted gurgle.

'A cruising speed of 45 mph can be maintained over long distances'. That statement alone recalls to me a totally different way of life!

120 A delicious thing of heavy metal that somehow never quite made the grade in the sophisticated sphere of Grand Prix racing. The history of the water cooled supercharged vee four AJS dates back to 1935, when an air cooled version, introduced at the Olympia Show, was presented as a basically road going machine with a super-sports tag. Provision was made for the fitting of a supercharger if required. Such AJSs were raced by the works with a 'blower' during 1936, including the TT races, but with little success. 1937 was a non-year for the 500cc overhead camshaft vee four, although in the following year road-holding problems had been solved, but the engine had a marked tendency to overheat. As was the case with so many projects halted by the start of World War II, the now water cooled version had at last proved itself to be a fairly reliable ultra fast racing machine, only to be axed in September 1939. Golden moments remembered when the mighty beast had turned in the first 100 mph lap of the Ulster Grand Prix at Clady in the month of August, just thirty eight years ago

121 Not everyone's choice of mount: one was either a Rudge fan or not. Having said that, I will quickly add that the Ulster model was one of the most delectable fast sporting mounts of the thirties particularly. For about £80 - a mint of money in 1937 - one bought a machine of 499cc [85mmx88mm] with four overhead valves, in which the exhaust pair were radially situated in the head, while the inlet were in parallel position. A positive stop foot change assembly was fitted directly to the four speed gearbox, while the QD rear wheel was indeed very quickly detachable. The large hand lever as seen in this picture, just above the 'R' on the primary chain case, was used to actuate the centre stand when required. A very similar model Ulster, tested by one of *Motor Cycling*'s staff men in 1939, achieved a top speed of just 94 mph at Brooklands. Graham Walker won the 1928 Senior Ulster Grand Prix on a four valve Rudge, hence the name

122 [*Right*] With the revival of interest in the songs and films of George Formby, younger enthusiasts may be pleased to learn that George was a very dedicated motorcycling type. Shown for the first time in 1935, one of George's better known films, *No Limit*, was a comedy based on the TT races of that year, with the song *Riding in the TT races*.

With an eye for classic machines of a sporting nature, Formby divided his affections between Ariel Square Fours and Nortons, and he is seen here with his remarkable wife Beryl just after collecting a new overhead camshaft International Norton in July 1947 from the Norton works at Bracebridge Street, Birmingham

123 [*Below*] While we rode about on our humble bangers, there was always time to stop and dream of greater stuff. To the impecunious enthusiast of the thirties the chances of ever owning such glorious beasties as the Vincent HRD were as remote as kicking a football to the moon.

Keen types are shown inspecting details of Phil Vincent's Series A 1000cc Rapide model in 1937. An entirely new motorcycle to the range of Stevenage made products, such a device would surely open an entirely new vista to motorcycling, with a 100 mph speed potential. Much thought had gone into the Rapide, and only best quality materials were used, while all fitting was carried out by very highly skilled staff, who lived motorcycles. Perhaps one weakness was the standard clutch assembly, which just was not up to transmitting the power from such a potent motor. Owners were given very strict instructions on how to use the clutch to avoid its malfunction.

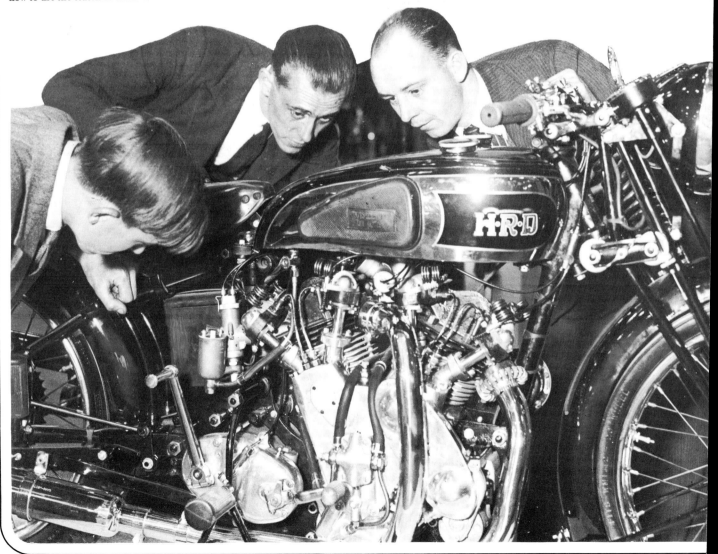

124 Time was when one admirer would suggest that SOS meant So Obviously Superior, yet another simply accepted that the bike he had seen ten minutes ago was 'Soss'. Perhaps correctly, the letters represented the trade name Super Onslow Special, its originator being the Midlands based constructor Vale Onslow. One must not exclude Tommy Meeton of New Malden, however, better known as an exponent on Francis Burnett machines, but having more than a little interest in the SOS, particularly in the later 1930s. With ten models in the programme for 1939, ranging from a wee 175 racing job to a 350 capable of hauling a sidecar with little fuss, all Villiers engined two strokes incidentally. Perhaps the most popular machine was the water cooled 250cc DW Club device [illustrated]. The very neatest of radiators was housed just below the tank nose. Ignition was by the well-known Villiers flywheel magneto system. A good speed for a 250cc two stroke in 1939, the SOS could be urged to approach 70 mph. One recalls that the Soss made a hissing noise in its going. Company slogan was 'The Mile A Minute Two-Stroke'

125 As long as I have been associated with motorcycles and motorcycling, time and time again the enthusiast has cried out for the ideal machine. The peculiar thing was - indeed still is - that when his wishes are granted he becomes wary of accepting anything new in principle. Pictured is the motorcycle sensation of 1939, the Brough Superior Golden Dream, being then the very last word in a series of 'perfect' machines built over a period of fifteen years by the Nottingham sportsman George Brough. Known only to produce the type of motorcycle that he himself would ever wish to own, Brough's interesting 'showman' character was always reflected in his super luxurious bikes. Valid boasts were 'I have only produced multi cylinder motorcycles to ensure smoothness of running' and 'No motorcycle, if it is to be good, can be cheap to buy'. For the Golden Dream, of which very few, perhaps only one was ever made, refinements were a horizontally opposed four cylinder ohv engine, shaft drive, plunger rear suspension, an easy hand operated centre stand, and electric starter. Last but never least was the high quality finish of every single part

126 As the motorcyclist clamours today for multi cylinder 'Superbikes', so did our clubmen and motorcycle 'nuts' of the later nineteen thirties yearn for a Triumph Speed Twin model. Launched in 1937, the Edward Turner designed 497cc overhead valve vertical twin set a new fashion in motorcycle engine development, important features being sweeter running and balance over other contemporary machines, and equal cooling of both cylinders. One weakness with these early Speed Twins was the possible departure of the cylinder block from its base flange, put down to insufficient 'meat' at that point, and only six studs to secure it to the crankcase. Later designs featured a considerably thicker cylinder base flange, plus eight studs, and no further trouble was experienced in that quarter. Capable of about 90 mph, the Speed Twin found great favour with the sophisticated rider who cared to cover long distances in comfort, while its distinctive exhaust note somehow heralded a new era in the pursuit of motorcycling

127 The simple little Villiers engined Coventry Eagle of 172cc typifies the average utility two stroke of our boyhood days, all a'hissing and often leaving more than a trace of smoke as it went its way. The kind of machine that 'Mother was quite happy to let us have to start us on our motorcycling career'. Pioneers of pressed steel construction for their lightweight machines, the Coventry Eagle concern were soon to find that German motorcycle firms were not slow in employing similar manufacturing techniques. The system could afford a basic, functional and indeed strong assembly.

As today, when still two stroke manufacturers will debate the best method of lubrication, be it petroil mixture or separate oiling, many Villiers engines of pre-war days used the unique automatic pressure system. By a series of connecting pipes between oil tank and crankcase, the latter serving as a pressure chamber in the course of the two cycle design, oil was forced by air pressure from its container [in the picture, just beneath the rear of the fuel tank] to the engine as the load demanded. Naturally, air leakage was the only bogey in an otherwise clever principle

128 A new Scott model for 1939, the 600cc Clubman's Special. One recalls the sporting scene during the late thirties when the very gods of club life owned the super fast Triumph Tiger 100 or Speed Twin models, or indeed an International Norton. The dedicated Scott type cried out for a model that would stay with the lads on club runs and where cruising could be enjoyed in the seventies and eighties. The Scott works at Shipley obliged, producing a sporty, albeit rather heavy device, following the normal water cooled twin two stroke fashion of Scotts, but a mite tougher in the engine department, particularly the crank assembly. Two Pilgrim pumps were fitted, one on each crankcase door, the offside instrument pumping oil to the main bearings, while the nearside one ensured that the cylinder walls should never be thirsty. The sprung heel was an optional extra, and an original design from a Wembley engineer who had sold the patent to Scotts during the mid-thirties. When road tested by the motorcycle press, the Clubman's Special had attained a speed of 94 mph at Brooklands

129 If we attempt to put the clock back, we cannot succeed for somehow things never appear to work out, in the very atmosphere of the time of their actual happening. Perhaps it is best left as just a glorious fireside memory! The very early post-war period, and many old marques of the motorcycle industry appeared again in a peacetime setting. *Motor Cycling*'s Editor, Graham Walker, visits the Vincent HRD works at Stevenage and goes for a 'romp', as we used to say, on Phil Vincent's new Series B 1000cc Rapide model in 1947. All the dash of a very special way of life is depicted here, with trousers tucked into a decent pair of socks, reversed cap and a pair of Mk VIII goggles [ex-RAF, 8/6d a pair].

A much more cobby affair than the pre-war Series A twin, the most obvious difference was the absence of a front down tube, the leading cylinder being employed to serve the purpose of this former item. No frame existed in the usual sense although an immensely strong box section beam passed from the steering head to a point amidships of the machine and to which the power unit was attached

130 Yet again doth the noble 350cc KTT Velocette appear and indeed it must do, for here is a thing of classic feature and function all at one time. The ultimate development of the original overhead camshaft design, born Hall Green, Birmingham, 1924. Mentioned elsewhere in *Kaleidoscope of Motorcycles*, the Mk VIII model [featured] was first produced for sale to the racing man during 1939 and became one of the best production racing machines of all time. A limited number were produced after the war, the last being sold during 1950.

Noted for its superlatively good steering qualities and smooth punchy motor, a semi-works model provided Freddie Frith with TT wins in 1948 and 1949, plus countless Continental Grands Prix firsts

131 During the latter half of the 1930s the famous Rudge-Whitworth Company at Crow Lane, Coventry, had introduced a very nippy little 250 machine called the Rapid. The enthusiasts liked it, but called for a more sporting version, which made its debut during 1938 and was appropriately classified as the 250 Sports. The design was simple and attractive and featured a peppier two valve power unit, the radial four valve engines having been discontinued some years before. Typical of the immediate pre-war period is the upswept exhaust pipe, which somehow marked any motorcycle in the sports category, although one's girlfriend often suffered in silence with over-warm legs in those days. It will be noticed that the Rudge system of coupled brakes was incorporated on the model shown, in which the foot lever, when depressed, brought both front and rear brakes into operation. The gear change lever was fitted on the nearside of the machine which, at that time, was totally foreign to any British motorcycle. It was the 250 Sports which formed the basis of the highly successful machines raced by the Pike brothers in pre and post-war years

132 The two Phils, Irving [*left*] and Vincent, seated on the post-war prototype Vincent HRD Rapide model in October 1946. Differing in many important details from the pre-war version, there existed no longer a true frame, rather was there a box section unit, which also served as an oil tank, surrounded by the fuel tank. Brampton girder forks were attached to the forward end of the box, while the cylinder head of the leading pot was connected to its underside. In this way an immensely strong assembly was achieved. The patent spring frame, a feature, with subsequent variations, on all Vincent HRDs since 1928, pivoted about the rear of the gearbox, the spring units being accommodated neatly beneath the special Feridax dualseat. To eliminate the possibility of a burnt-out clutch, with so much power on tap from its 1000cc motor, as had been the case with the pre-war series A models, Phil Vincent had designed his own clutch assembly, with two stages of take-up, including a servo system. In practice, the faster the engine turned over, the tighter the clutch would grip. Vincent HRD: a classic motorcycle of all time with well maintained models today being of considerable value. A personal recollection of the exciting new Series was the writer Allan Chappelow's machine GU476 being the first London registered Vincent B in April 1947

133 Developed during the war years, and in many cases slung to a paratrooper's back, the famous Royal Enfield Flea, as it later became known, was a typical economical go-anywhere lightweight of the late nineteen forties. Simplicity itself, the 125cc single cylinder two stroke was of the conventional three port type, with flywheel magneto and direct lighting, thus no engine running, no lights. The pressed steel girder forks utilised a thick rubber band as a springing medium and I had never heard of anyone who had suffered from a broken elastic in thousands of miles of riding the Flea. Note the dinky little hand change assembly leading to the three speed gearbox, and the cold starting shutter on the air cleaner intake. One had to take great care in timing these little engines, which worked on a cam arrangement within the flywheel, or it was quite possible that, when starting up, the Flea would promptly charge off in a reverse direction, as I once learned to my cost!

134 Surprising to those who had only just received their demob suit, trilby and gratuity, that already Italy was arming up for future Grand Prix battles. The year: 1946, and the birth of the famous 'Gambalunga' [long leg] Moto-Guzzi. A 500cc single cylinder racing model, with the traditional Guzzi feature of a horizontally placed power unit, the 'long leg' tag came as a result of its fairly long stroke [90mm] compared with the bore of 84mm. Again, in keeping with previous designs from Mandello del Lario, the rear suspension system was novel with spring boxes situated beneath the crankcase, and not visible in the photograph. The scissors type dampers at the rear of this Guzzi could be adjusted by the fly nut shown. Strangely, after 1946 Moto-Guzzi reverted to the Brampton Girder front fork assembly, although the bottom link type of Guzzi's own manufacture, as we see here, were a standard fitting in later years. Following usual Guzzi principles of design, the 'frame' could be described as an amalgamation of pressings, plates and tubes. On the nearside of the machine was situated an outside flywheel

135 [Below] 1948 and all's well. A time when one could actually buy a British motorcycle and be assured that one was buying the finest product. In Harris tweed jacket [how many coupons?!] TT rider and Norton agent Harold Daniell casts an eye towards the beefy side valve power unit of a Model 16H, while the great Norton tuner Steve Lancefield [one of Harold's old buddies] sits astride the model.

Now the story goes that Harold was a testy old buffer and sometimes as unapproachable as the super racing Nortons that he rode to so many victories. My memories of HLD are, however, the very nicest ones, and whenever I visited his Forest Hill premises [seen here] I could only describe him as the kindest and most good humoured of men

OFFICES

136 The 'new' BSA of 1946. Possibly the most respected grandfather of all subsequent vertical twin cylinder designs to come from Armoury Road, Birmingham. Of 497cc capacity, and held by many to be the correct maximum capacity for any 360 degree parallel twin, this 'Beesa' employed push rod operated overhead valves, in which the rods passed through special tubes, situated between the two cylinders. A normal four speed gearbox was fitted, operated by a foot change assembly. An interesting feature was the centre stand, which was hooked down by the rider's toe, and retracted by the release of a special catch on the uppermost end of the seat pillar tube. The control just beneath the saddle operated the carburettor air slide. Later models of the A7, as it was soon to be listed, were fitted with BSA plunger type rear suspension units. You will hear many a true motorcyclist declare that this was the finest bike that BSA ever made. Standing about the twin in the picture, prior to its being despatched to the Paris Show, are, from left to right, S F Digby, BSA General Sales Manager, George Savage, Motorcycle Sales Manager and H Perkins, Designer

137 Peacetime manufacture of the famous 45 cubic inch [750cc] Harley Davidson once again.

This is the renowned side-valve model WL fashioned in pre-war days, later conscripted for military service to be classified as the WLA [A for Army] when finished in a substantial coat of olive green paint.

Detail improvements on this 1947 HD were what was described as a striking new name plate; streamlined instrument panel; high pressure oil circulating system and an improved circuit breaker adjustment. 'A dependable speedy motorcycle that makes an ideal mount for the conservative rider' went the sales literature of the time

MOTORCYCLING THE SPORT

138 Hard-worked Dobbin at the rear appears little concerned about the line-up of Triumph team riders for the 1914 ACU Six Days Trial. All astride the famous 550cc model, the worthies from left to right are, Albert Catt, Fred W Chapman, T J Ross, Billy Westwood and A Clayton.
Smiling for the cameraman here, although a very different matter when these competitors were faced with the rain and muddy conditions on Litton Slack which brought about a riders' strike

While there may be hundreds of nearing middle age gas inspectors who use a motorcycle
solely as a means of convenient transport, there are others who live for
spectating at or participating in events where motorcycles are engaged in competition.
Such has been the order since the early 1900's and there appears no evidence
that things are to change in this direction.
Being fast and highly manoeuvrable, the motorcycle lends itself very suitably for road or track racing,
yet, at a slower tempo, the perfect tool for climbing a rugged and demanding section of trials going.
Speedway and Moto Cross are most worthy additions to the list of motorcycle sports.
While genuinely not wishing to criticise the current scene, however,
specialisation of machinery in certain areas of the game, plus monetary rewards
often far too great in relation to the effort made by competitors, has removed the essential spirit of sportsmanship.
Time was when courage and hard work provided a healthy balance to things.

139 Location: Luton Hoo. Event: Speed Trials. Date: July 1920. A magnificent entry of 200 riders assembled on a fine but blustery day although the field telephone linking the start and finish lines did get a little temperamental. A speed shot here is of A G Gripper, complete with pipe, of course, well down to things on his stripped-for-action Zenith Gradua.

Champions of the meeting were Howard Davies [AJS] and George Dance [Sunbeam], who were described as the '17 secs merchants'. An amusing moment was enjoyed by the crowd in the first sidecar event when Davies collected a small boy as passenger and packed him, laying face downwards, in the sidecar, with the result that, as he passed, nothing of the sidecar's occupant could be seen but two small feet

140 Respected by those who cannot claim to be remotely associated with motorcycles or motorcycling, the classic Scott Squirrel and owner were given *carte blanche* in any circles. Lined up in a typical Yorkshire street in the early twenties are, from left to right, W Guy, Clarrie Wood and Geoffrey Hill, participants in a 1000 mile trial over some of the severest roads in England. When this picture was taken, Alfred Angas Scott, the creator of such a remarkable marque, had deserted the motorcycle in favour of marine and motorcar engines. The two speed [foot operated] twin cylinder, water cooled two strokes were, at this time, still very much a Mr Scott type Scott, however. With the passing of AAS in 1923, following an attack of pneumonia, contracted during a pot holing incident, the Scott became the product of lesser minds, as one old engineer hastened to advise me several years ago. Regardless of such comment, which may well contain more than an element of truth, the Scott still remains much the motorcycle that is different

141 A peculiarly handsome motorcycle of the old days was the NUT, built, one may correctly guess, by the Newcastle-Upon-Tyne Motor Company.,

Most times fitted with side-valve vee twin power units of 500cc and above, the quality machines were finished in a distinctive nut brown colour with gold lining in appropriate places. A traditional feature of the Hugh Mason designed NUT was the cylindrical fuel tank, clamped to the machine's top tube with two neatly drilled bands.

On parade here is the official works trials team with chain driven models of the early 1920s. Note the spare inner tubes wrapped around the handlebars of XR1 and XR3, and what better place for quick removal when required in the event of a severe puncture during the heat of trials going

142 'My dear boy, I am enclosing a photograph taken at our Inter Varsity Hill Climb, Aston Clinton, nr Tring, during March 1925.....' You may at first be amused by the scene, so very different from your own, but I think, with detailed study of the picture, perhaps impressed! You will observe that the road surface is very different from the present sophisticatedly rolled tar macadam, but you may rest assured we enjoyed ourselves, even with solid framed machines and girder forks. In order to lighten our motorcycles, we would often remove the saddle and substitute with one of Aunt Kitty's cushions. Norton mounted competitor Number 14 has done just that. Unusual is the HRD, in the centre of the picture, for it has Druid pattern front forks fitted which, to my knowledge, were not standard on Howard Davies' models. Of course, Davies had previously ridden AJS with Druid forks and this may have been a Special. Please allow for the fact that the years may have clouded my memory!

143 A trio of mid-twenties Ner-a-Cars. Whether the designer, American C A Neracher, intended at the very outset to produce a two wheeled vehicle which would indeed be near a car in concept and appearance, perhaps we shall never know, although roadholding, steering and general weather protection were more in line with the automobile. Original English versions of Ner-a-Car were made by the Sheffield Simplex concern at Kingston-on-Thames and sported a box section chassis, more than a frame, hub centre steering, and a 285cc two stroke engine with a novel form of friction drive. Transmission engagement was operated by a special quick action twist grip control on the left handlebar. From personal experience, the first ride ever on such a Ner-a-Car was a mite 'hairy' with such a control. Later products from Kingston-on-Thames used a side valve Blackburne engine with a more conventional 'gearbox' and riders, from left to right, Hadfield, Brennon and Lush, are seated on such models in trials trim

144 Dirt track racing or speedway, as it was later to be known, possessed a very special atmosphere. Possibly at its very height of popularity during the late 20s and through all the years of the 30s, immense crowds as yet unspoilt by television and all the vulgar issues of this tragic day, cheered on their idols beneath powerful lights, cinder dust and the truly glorious whiff of racing fuels and oils.

Eventually, as with most things, too much specialisation crept into speedway, resulting in one machine looking little different from the next. The Rudge started it all by becoming the most suitable bike for the job in hand. This 1932 model is, however, a special Rudge in which the crankcase has been turned round, together with the cylinder barrel, so that the push rods cannot be seen here. It is presumed that the operation took place in order to avoid a countershaft drive for the transmission system of the single speed model, for the primary drive is on the offside of the Rudge. The front forks are typical 'Speedway Webbs'

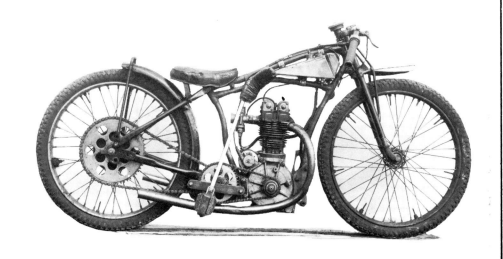

145 Nearly every motorcycle manufacturer jumped on the dirt track machine bandwagon not least Scotts, who would again provide a plot so very different from anything else which stood two wheels and engine amidships. By 1929 the cobby little Speedway Special Scott appeared based on a bike used by ace rider Frank Varey a few years before. The power unit was a well tuned TT type, laced to a three speed gearbox, although for small track racing the machine was permanently held in second gear. The diminutive radiator for the water cooled system was a joy to behold, while the little barrel container on the down tube possessed two compartments, one for the fuel and the other for lubricant. This prototype Speedway Scott is fitted with forks from a standard model, to be replaced soon after by the special forks manufactured by the famous Birmingham firm of H C Webb and Company.

146 Club types and friends obviously enjoying themselves, yet not appearing to disturb Arthur Hornbeam's domestic fowls over the way in their wooden mansion.

The new sport of turf surfing in progress, although I cannot help feeling that those rear mudguard stays must have offered more than an occasional groan with at least a 16 stone load to pull.

Nearest the camera is one of the only twin port single cylinder four strokes made by Velocette, the KTP model with coil ignition. Produced during the extreme Depression year of 1931, the KTP was an honest attempt to provide a sporting overhead camshaft motorcycle for the hard-up enthusiast. For some peculiar reason, the model never 'took on' and was considered far from a real Velocette by the motorcycling fraternity. Perhaps it was the coil ignition, or those twin exhaust pipes. Perhaps it reminded too many of Depression motorcycling, with an attendant stigma!

147 When enthusiasm ran high in motorcycle club life. Just outside *The Wake Arms*, Epping, in the early thirties, an official gives final briefing to some sixty motorcyclists from various London clubs, before their departing on a Sporting Run. The competition was open to solo riders only, who had to cover a hazardous course of eighty miles for the Kempton Cup.

A sad reflection on the present state of the British motorcycle industry, when one may spot in this picture alone more than six different makes of 'home grown' machines.

Typical of the period, the motorcyclists are wearing the heavy black rubber competition coats or variations of the current flying rig. Many of us will mourn the passing of the cloth cap for motorcycling, I am sure. As life was hard, sporting get-togethers were more than appreciated, and no Sunday morning only five mile trips for the majority of motorcycles, indeed they were hard working everyday machines and showed honest evidence of it. Note the rain-shedder on the AJW, still correct twenty years later on this make

48 An accepted fact that the better type of person attended race meetings at Donington, and where most individuals could, in confidence, show a clear set of front teeth. Severe but true. In a beautiful parkland setting, racing of a very high standard took place. Our picture was taken in 1933 from the steep hill, high above the hairpin, which indeed became less and less acute, as the track was widened and cut away at that point over the years.

The shout has gone up that the massed start 500cc race is underway, and Tom and Alice, in the centre of the photograph, are quickly rushing to their feet, while other leather coated enthusiasts have taken to the trees in order to gain a better viewing advantage.

During the latter part of 1937 the start/finish area was moved to the far side of the course, near Redgate corner, years when sophistication moved in in a big way at Donington

49 Cadwell Park in all its glory! I must confess that the picture has really foxed me, for I am not quite sure whether this sidecar and three wheeler event took place in the immediate pre or post-war period, as the racing scene was, in those times, so very much the same. Described as a truly miniature TT circuit, Cadwell Park, set in the beautiful, albeit flat countryside near Louth, in Lincolnshire, was originally only about a mile in length, although in more recent years some considerable extensions have been made, bringing the course near to full Grand Prix dimensions. Note how the Morgan's passenger manages to supply a smile as he places his weight over its tail prior to rocketing up the 'mountain', while the two Norton outfits are about to corner in the wake of the heady fumes of burnt Castrol 'R' from the Morgan. Perhaps one may be permitted to say in all honesty that 'those were the days', and a visit to Cadwell was so much an exciting experience. A time of less sophistication, and an abundance of truly great characters, who more than often rode their racing machines to the meetings

150   I knew you when I was a youth
You were the very thing that every full-blown
speedman held in awe
Sometimes you posed for shots left, right and
centre, or down the line. Box Brownies clicked
and schoolboy voices called for more.
Some said your racing JAP displaced far in
excess of nine nine eight ccs, indeed, the plus-
foured know-all of our club declared 'one two
four six'....
But then you changed your engine be it once
or twice, deep you were, deep as the mighty
whale of Melville's boiling seas.
Perhaps you presently reside where last I saw
you in the North, perhaps on fine summer
days your pilot is still inclined to give you all
the stick....
Oh rorty beast, please thunder till the end,
there's never been a bus quite like you, Moby
Dick.
    The Brough Superior featured is much in
the stamp of big Brough competition
machinery as Moby Dick, but is presumed to
be a reworked version of Jack Carr's famous
Pendine Sands racer, here trimmed for road
use

151   Way up on the Yorkshire Moors at
Blubberhouses, and the 20th Annual Scott
Trial, November 1937. Originally a test of
both man and machine's ability to complete
rough going against the clock for Scott motorcycles and employees of the Bradford Works
[1914], the event was later extended to include
any make of motorcycle and any competitor.
    A keen gathering of very respectable
looking motorcyclists watch a Levis rider
being given a welcome shove at the Kex Beak
section. The Levis was a very popular cross
country machine during the later thirties, its
manufacturers, Butterfields of Stetchford,
having produced good quality lightweight two
strokes only until 1927. Four stroke models
were something of a departure from former
policy, therefore. Although pretty basic in
engine design, the overhead valve Levis, its
push rods contained in one tube, was well
made and something of a notorious thumper,
with a stroke of about 112mm. Note the
pilgrim pump mounted on the timing case, all
part of the total loss lubrication system

152   Square but certainly true should I say
that there were so many things infinitely more
pleasurable in the motorcycle game during the
pre-war period than is the present circus.
Even if Trials machines were the very last
word in sophistication for the job in hand,
they at least retained more than an identity
with road machines, albeit 'sporty boys' type.
No screaming, unbearably noisy anti-social
devices, rather classic bikes, British and
undeniably best. Seated on examples of
machinery that once were the very envy of all
foreign manufacturers are 100% AJS star
George Rowley [centre], Jack Williams [right]
and Vic Brittain on Norton overhead camshaft
International mdoels, fitted with all kinds of
niceties such as plunger spring heels and what
would be later referred to as 'Manx' tanks.
The scene: eve of the 1938 International Six
Days Trial start at Llandrindod Wells. Great
Britain won the trophy, while Germany won
the vase. Alas, we have failed miserably in
recent years - could it be the bikes, could it be
the men?

153 [Above] I will never accept that there can exist anything superior to immaculate black racing leathers and the truly remarkable 'pudding basin' helmet. Can we honestly say that we have progressed to higher standards with current racing garb being all colours of the rainbow, and those quite ridiculous helmets more the wear of astronauts? Witness this delightful shot of riders engaged in a 350cc class battle at Donington Park during April 1939, and the classic combination of a well kitted Mk VII Velocette competitor, J Garnett [43] and his unfaired machine.

Alas, by the mid 1960's the quite vulgar trendy disease caught on in the motorcycle racing world, and with it riding styles became ragged and ill disciplined. Peculiar attitudes towards race organisers became the order at every meeting of note, with often a point blank refusal to ride should some obstacle around the course offend any rider. I wonder sometimes if these riders ever bothered to consider their moral obligations to the paying customers who, in many cases, would ride miles to watch their idols in action

154 [Left] Whichever way my remark may be interpreted, I would caption this Southampton quayside shot taken in July 1938.... 'Before the rot set in'. The scene is of a section of two army teams of storm troopers who had come to represent their native Germany for the International Six Days Trial centred around Llandrindod Wells. Other than the three British machines making the front rank, and no doubt ridden by officials who had come to greet the German competitors, nearly all the other motorcycles in evidence are BMW horizontally opposed twin cylinder jobs, with a few NSUs to the rear, and one lightweight DKW two stroke, Number 6. In the very centre of the photograph is Georg Meier, wearing that classic item of Continental headgear of pre-war days, the white linen wind-cap. It will also be recalled that a year later in 1939 Meier became the first foreign rider to win the Senior TT, riding on that occasion a supercharged BMW model

155 The great DKW/EMC controversy. Although producing a very interesting 350cc split single two stroke design during the late nineteen forties, the remarkable Dr Joseph Ehrlich, may we say, achieved anything but popularity when he entered what appeared to be genuine production racer 250cc DKW machines as EMCs [Ehrlich Motor Cycles] in races during the early post-war years. Wherever the EMCs were down to race, inevitably there were heated scenes of disgruntled competitors complaining that the bikes were, in fact, true German RSS or SS model forced induction DKWs. Pressing on regardless, Dr Ehrlich insisted that his machines were EMC, and they would race under such a name. Pictured is the late David Whitworth aboard an 'EMC' at Oliver's Mount, Scarborough road races in 1947, on which he won the 250cc event.

156 [Below] 1947 and a Great Britain at peace, the first TT races for seven long years and many of the great characters of the game back in the Isle of Man. Who else but the great little Charles Markham with that famous cloth cap and Mk VIIIs, taking the post-war version of the International Norton for a pleasant canter. As editorial staffman for *Motor Cycling*, Charles will always be remembered for his very special style of journalistic writing and those remarkable little thumbnail sketches which often showed him in some amusing predicament, mostly with his two speed Scott and enquiring policemen.

The Norton thumps along the Glencrutchery Road, a beautiful beast now fitted with the famous Roadholder telescopic front forks, while Markham no doubt thinks of suitable qualicatives to describe his impressions in the 'Green 'un'

157 Evidence, dear readers, that there was once a time when no wretched safety neurosis existed to spoil the simplicity of just riding a motorbike as one felt inclined. At ten miles an hour or 90, skill was the thing that ensured one remained a whole body at the conclusion of a run. Phil Heath is obviously enjoying the moment to its full as he speeds the Inter Norton along a section of the Isle of Man Course during a 'rest' period between races in 1947. The International model in its post-war guise was to enjoy several wins in the special IOM races for clubmen on sports machines, as opposed to out-and-out TT bikes. Later the Gold Star BSA became 'king' in both Junior and Senior classes

158 [Below] 'Breasting the Mountain', Cadwell Park, 1946. Surprisingly, road racing got back into its stride so very quickly after World War II, and if my memory serves me correctly Cadwell fixtures were the very first in the firing order of things. This action picture of Tommy Wood, aviating his Erswood Special, typifies the immediate post-war racing scene which really was so little different from all that had been enjoyed until 1939. Tommy, of course, was a pre-war rider, mostly on Velocette machines, and had been the cat's pyjamas at Cadwell Park and Alexandra Palace. The Erswood was essentially a short circuit bike and had been put together in nine hours. The frame and forks were basically MSS Velocette, and the power unit a 500cc JAP. Mike Erskine and Wood had built the racer, and little intelligence will be necessary to appreciate how such a device got its name. The Tommy Wood/Erswood combination won many races, although some enthusiasts will recall more clearly when Tommy rode works Moto-Guzzis in later years. He won the 1951 Lightweight TT on such a marque

That Delightful Engineering Monstrosity the Sidecar Outfit

To find a joy of living when seated about a conglomeration of tubes connecting a sidecar to a motorcycle
and not forgetting the famous swan-neck attachment 'up front', plus, where certain corners are encountered,
having us calling for the Lord to receive our souls, defies reason.
Such a picture will be appreciated by anyone who has ridden a motorcycle outfit at a sporting gait.
If we ask the Lord to deliver us in one piece it may well be that we have been faced
with a left-hand corner of adverse camber on the road of our delight.
The sidecar is void of any weighty passenger at the time.
At this stage of the proceedings, a cool head is most definitely required
with a prayer that if the sidecar wheel 'comes up' there is sufficient turn remaining in the throttle control
to accelerate the motorcycle around the sidecar. If we are favoured on this occasion
it will have the effect of bringing the wheel down again.

60 Designed to be attached to an ordinary pedal cycle, this quaint device was, in fact, a sidecar incorporating a small two-stroke Metro engine. Ingenious thinking, 1914 style! Drive was by chain to a countershaft situated behind the motor. On the end of this shaft was fixed a pulley, providing a belt final drive to the sidecar wheel.

There were two control levers situated on the handlebars, one operating the carburettor and the other actuating the engine decompressor. Although this model was single-geared and designed for use as a runabout or in level country, a variable gear version was later made available.

Maker's suggestion to all owners: in the event of a breakdown, the pedal cycle should be detached and ridden to nearest garage

61 [Right] Tasteful BSA advertisement of 1920 in which the motorcycle and, in this case, sidecar to accompany it are treated in the correct perspective. How things have changed in recent years! The motorcycle appears to be of the type with vee twin engine of 770cc no doubt, deeply valanced mudguards and the dummy belt rim system of front wheel braking.

At one time the BSA Company produced their own sidecars, luxurious affairs in which a passenger might travel with some dignity and in the event of adverse weather conditions as suggested in the advertisement, there existed delicious things as the Easting screen. Now this fitment served on fine days as a simple yet effective windshield, but as soon as the rain clouds gathered, the whole thing could be raised up and over the head of the passenger. Price ... £4.10.0 and immediate delivery guaranteed

59 [Left] Built by one of the pioneers of the British motorcycle industry, Phelon and Moore of Cleckheaton, Yorkshire, the P&M, later to be called the Panther, achieved great popularity with the family sidecar man. Early versions were of side valve pattern, although overhead valves soon replaced the former system, its makers convinced that hard slogging and a good performance could go hand in hand with well thought out design. One characteristic feature on all 'Big Pussys', as they were affectionately referred to, was the sloping position of the cylinder. Smaller versions of the Panther, rated at 248cc, again with a forwardly inclined engine, were sold in their thousands to the young man who had to consider every penny, and a visit to Pride and Clarke, if one had £27.10.0 to spare could ensure purchase of a fully equipped job during those glorious days of the thirties. We are here treated to the gentle picture of the 'new' P&M of 1920 with sidecar attached. For some reason, our canine friend has decided that to be close to the mistress is by far the best place

162 Shorten the two names Dunford and
Elliott and, with a little bit of letter re-
arrangement, hey presto, we have Dunelt.
Pioneers of the larger capacity two stroke, the
first Dunelt appeared during 1919 and was of
500cc.

A sales slogan of the time was 'Pull? Yes,
pull anything', for these Birmingham made
two strokes employed a unique system in
which a truncated piston, larger at its base,
improved considerably both breathing and
scavenging sequences. With such apparent
efficiency, the Dunelt was ideally suited for
sidecar work and speed with good fuel
consumption figures which were very credit-
able.

The 1921 model as shown is typical of the
fairly uncomplicated motorcycle of the
twenties, with its simple bolt-on gearbox and
chain cum belt transmission. The front forks
are, however, of great interest, for they were
only attached at one 'serious' point, that being
at the bottom of the steering head. The upper
end of the fork blades were left free to operate
against a large laminated spring, which can
just be seen here

163 With such a motorcycle as the Scott
being on the road to a British institution in its
time, one wonders why an Uncle Sam
character appears to give his impression of
what water cooling is all about. Was there
some subtle reason for US that the artist had
in mind?

Typical of the standard model Scott of
1920, the advertisement features a two-speed
job of either 486 or 532cc, fitted with the very
advanced telescopic forks for the period.

Full triangulation for all tubes in both
motorcycle and sidecar chassis structures,
such a principle was to remain strictly Scott
practice while its designer remained in office.
Alfred Scott's personal transport was a 1913
outfit 'AK18', very little different from the one
in this illustration

Watercooled!!
Scott

WRITE FOR ILLUSTRATED BROCHURE AND NAME OF NEAREST AGENT TO -

The Scott Motor Cycle Co. Ltd.   SALTAIRE. YORKSHIRE

164 Now what could be nicer than this? A comfortable gentleman on an equally comfortable looking outfit, crossing a ford in the Hertfordshire countryside, AD 1920.

Although we have just missed the 8hp Blackburne engined Rex as it chuffles its pleasant way, we might just catch a glimpse of the belt rim on the rear wheel. We must ask of DU869's owner, 'How come, sir, with belt drive you are experiencing no slipping under the watery conditions?', to which Oswald will no doubt reply, 'Wide pulley centres, dear boy'.

Observe the step situated between machine and sidecar, the means of entry to the latter being through the 'passage'

165 'In that special pre-dusk moment when we would walk from the high ground to remotely situated farmhouses where many a fine tea was enjoyed for 10d' - thus did J B Priestley so finely describe the charactered pleasure of a life in his native Yorkshire.

Pictured rounding The Stake is the unique brainchild of A A Scott, the Sociable or 'Crab', during September 1920. Although originator of very advanced motorcycles, with models winning both the 1912 and 1913 TTs, Scott appeared to lose interest in motorcycle design after the First World War, turning his technical brilliance towards marine engines and the strange looking three wheeler. With a chassis built up from a complex of tubes, the Crab was powered by a 578cc water cooled twin two stroke engine which employed rotary valves. Hub steering at the single front wheel was another advanced feature.

It is said that the vehicle's lop-sided appearance did little to attract potential buyers and as with so many other unorthodox designs the whole project was shelved in but a few years

166   A nippy little job would be the best way to describe E B Ware's twin cylinder side valve Morgan, winner of the first Light Car Long Handicap at Brooklands, 24th March 1920. At the risk of offending those Morganatics who worship the very oil droppings from the unique three wheelers, my memories of these devices were nostalgic, but could not cloud my views that much in the construction of Morgans left a great deal to be desired. Perhaps the late H F S Morgan employed the same line of thinking as Ettore Bugatti, working on the principle that the strictly functional took complete precedence over frill. For all of that, the Morgan, especially the little two speeder, was a delightful thing to drive, the power to weight ratio providing a veritable sting of performance. To those remembering for a moment or two their days of delight, shoe-horned into a Moggie, the experience was not far removed from flying on terra firma

167   As American as July 4th or apple pie, the big twin Indian motorcycle must rank as a classic piece for all time. Brimming over with very advanced features, the Indian of a post-Great War period possessed a spring frame, electric starter and lights plus what are referred to as clean handlebars with but two hand twist grip controls [carburettor and ignition]. This 1000cc Powerplus model was ideally suited for sidecar work and such outfits appeared regularly in early silent films with characters like the Keystone Cops proceeding at enormous speed in pursuit of some equally amusing subject. By 1921 the Powerplus had been superseded by the Chief model of fond memory

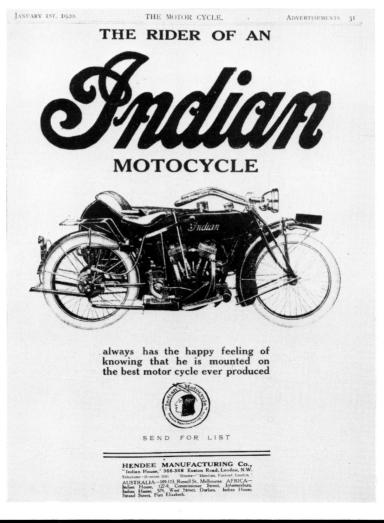

168 When not an Indian, then the Harley Davidson of which a well-used example here serves to transport a 13th Century knight to the Collingham [Leeds] Open Air Day some fifty years ago.

Characteristic of the early Harley Davidson motorcycles was the valve arrangement in which the inlet valve was of the pushrod operated overhead type, while the exhaust item sat at the side of the cylinder. Note the cut-away in the fuel tank to permit the overhead valve rocker to have sufficient working clearance and, of course, to permit easy plug changes when necessary.

The excellent Harley front forks were later fitted in modified form to Brough Superiors

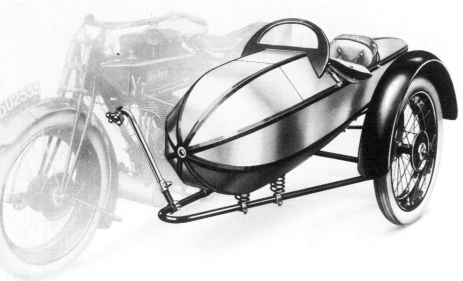

169 Such was society's attitude to the motorcycle and sidecar type in the nineteen twenties and thirties that if the set-up was of a sporting nature, one was accepted. If, however, the utterly reliable and perhaps even a little plodding family man chuffed his side valve way to a Sunday afternoon coast with a capacious henhouse full of children, he was not quite 'correct' for sophisticated company. In all honesty, however, some of the family sidecars were better talked of than seen, but who could resist the Aero style single seat jobs, dashing things in any circle of sensible people.

In cricket sweater, cord breeches, long stockings and brogues, young Herbert, pipe in mouth, waited impatiently outside 'Ivydene' on his Rudge with Zepplein sidecar. In a few minutes the lovely Millicent would be his for this summer's afternoon. 'Step inside, my darling, and place your heavenly bottom on the pneumatic cushions.' They returned by the light of the moon!

170 Originally to be operated by ex-servicemen only, the first motorcycle taxis appeared in that up-to-date city of Nottingham in July 1920. The fare paid: one shilling for the first mile and eightpence for any mile afterwards. Note the meter well in evidence for, in this case, a lady passenger!

The motorcycle is a Campion with big JAP 6hp engine of which six were purchased by the city authorities for this specialised work. Such was the success of the outfits that when suitably adapted they were much in favour with commercial travellers of the period.

Clearly seen is the leather hood and celluloid windscreen of the sidecar, while side-screens could be fitted when necessary to afford complete waterproofing. With two passengers, these Campion motorcycle taxis could ascend the steepest hills in second gear, and generally were found to be much handier than the ordinary taxi cab

171 A few years ago, a party of Vintagents assembled on Horse Guards Parade literally to ride or drive into Europe, as part of Great Britain's 'contribution' to her entry to the EEC. Of the sidecar brigade, Bob Thomas, from the Isle of Man, had entered a Douglas outfit, very similar to the one shown in our picture and boasting of a TT history. Viewing the device at very close quarters, I found it hardly possible to appreciate that such a frail looking set-up could have been wrenched around the tortuous Island course at racing speeds to finish 'well up', as is said. This 1923 sidecar TT shot shows fourth place finisher D H Davidson with his 596cc horizontally opposed flat twin model. Points of interest are the experimental Research Association disc brakes, sprung sidecar wheel and a set of spare plugs situated on the fuel tank nose. Davidson will be remembered by many an old timer as the man who was first to lap Brooklands Track at over 100 mph, on that occasion mounted on a solo Harley Davidson. There was no business or family connection in the name Davidson - purely coincidence!

172 In my early motorcycling years I was brought up on tales of all the great characters of the sport and their various exploits. Some accounts are fit to print, others not. Second only to the great Ted Baragwanath in brute strength, when handling mighty vee-twin engined monsters, was the immortal George Patchett, who, it was said, could remove and replace a tyre and tube on any motorcycle wheel with never the need to use levers. I certainly believe it.

Competing in the Welsh TT of 1927, Patchett used a JAP powered McEvoy outfit and just look at those wheels. The plot is sliding beautifully, with the rear wheel churning up some of Pendine's sands, while the passenger is doing his best to get as much weight over the bike as possible. In later years, G W Patchett designed much of the Czechoslovakian Jawa TT machines, as well as acting as engineering consultant to many British motorcycle manufacturers.

Alas, with the passing of these great characters so has gone the equally great British motorcycle industry - as harmful a fact as it is sad

173 A luxury Scott in the form of the Reynolds Special for 1932. Much in the fashion of the customisers [horrible word] of today, who intend to improve a factory product, Liverpudlian Albert Reynolds selected the trim little Sprint Special Scott with single down tube frame to form the basis of his specialised model, spoken of as 'a Scott for connoisseurs'. Built up from carefully selected parts and beautifully fitted, the specification 'available' consisted of 500 or 600cc engines, high or low compression pistons as required, and standard or close ratio gears. Brampton bottom link forks were a typical Reynolds feature, as was the Velocette foot change assembly, 'Master' spring heel, 'pear drop' header tanked radiator, specially flared petrol tank and mudguards. The special pan saddle provided comfort hitherto unknown to the long distance rider. Of the two headlamps fitted, the nearside one could be independently operated for 'dimming operations'. With a Noxal Launch sidecar body fitted on a Swallow spring-wheel chassis [as illustrated], the complete outfit 'as luxurious as a modern car' sold for £160

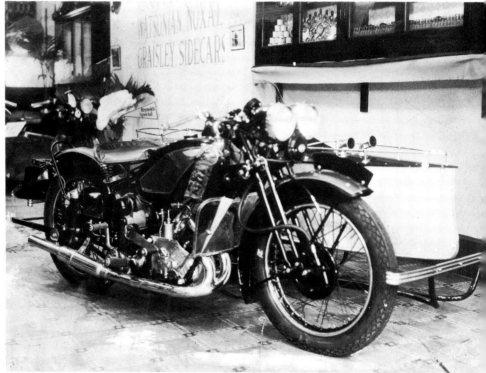

174 The war against the motor bandit is nothing new. Today the forces of the law have more to contend with, that is the difference.

During the early thirties, an enterprising Hampton Court based company produced this sturdy sidecar to act as a mobile watch-out 'tower'. The vertical board amidships is in fact a back rest for two guards, who sat facing forward and rearward respectively, to enable them to maintain an uninterrupted view of the road both ways. Quick to appreciate the advantages of such a device in order to deal with acts of banditry on the highway, the Spanish Government ordered twenty five of these outfits for their armed road patrols. A contemporary report stated that the introduction in England of these special sidecars would be a definite move towards the defeat of the motor bandits.

Here we see an outfit undergoing preliminary tests at Brooklands in September 1932

175 Overworked words to describe the exploits of competition sidecarists, such as 'blasting' or 'storming' appear never to be given rest in modern motorcycle journalism. I will, therefore, suggest that appropriate words of substitution to caption this rear view of two German army competitors in conflict with Welsh terrain near Babel during 1938 might be 'they purposefully attack'. Never missing an opportunity to test, test and re-test the capabilities of men, machinery and equipment for a war that became inevitable, the International Six Days Trial provided more than a rehearsal for the German entrants. So soon would BMW outfits such as this be finished in olive green, with crews wearing the never to be forgotten Stahlhelm for serious business

76 [*Above left*] Kim Collett 'all out' on a
sprint Norton and sidecar in March 1933.
Collett will, of course, be remembered as one
of the early Donington Park and Syston
sidecar stars and pioneer of the special racing
Norton engines of 596cc. Although not
absolutely sure of my facts regarding the birth
of the overhead camshaft 600, it was known
that Collett originally used bored out 588cc
Model 19 power units which were push rod
operated, although the late Harold Taylor
advised me that many 490 [79x100] overhead
camshaft engines had their stroke extended to
113mm by private owners to give a capacity of
nearly 600cc. In this superb picture where
Collett's passenger adopts a typical Brooklands 'fully horizontal', I will risk suggesting
that the engine here shown is a straight 490cc
overhead camshaft unit. When Nortons
produced their own 'Cammy' 600 in both
racing and official Trials forms, the top tube
of the frames were built with a decided vertical
'kink' in order to accept a very tall engine.
The period of manufacture was about 1938

77 [*Left*] Those were the days when real
people with the nicest tendency of being
unspoilt enjoyed themselves in comparatively
simple pleasure. Members of the Horsham
Motor Cycle Club are here picnicking near the
Sussex coast. The style of dress of the adults
might suggest a just pre World War One
setting, as indeed the motorcycle outfits tend
to do, although the smiling lad in the process
of eating a biscuit somehow looks early 1920s.
One suspects that Grandma in the centre of
the group knows a thing or two!

178 [*Above*] Mark, learn and very much
digest is my directive to all those who presently
race sidecar outfits in vintage events. What
better example of an immediate post-war
Norton/Watsonian combination can be shown
than this overhead camshaft 596cc job that
took Eric Oliver and Denis Jenkinson to world
champion honours in three wheeler races
during the late forties and very early fifties.
Although most of us associate the Manx
Norton with engine capacities of either 350 or
500cc, some ten of nearly 600cc were built,
primarily intended for sidecar racing alone.
The frame and forks of pukka Norton 'bigger
banger' jobs were considerably heavier in
general construction than the solo racing
mounts, in order to accept the greater stresses
that sidecar hauling in competition events
imposed. To me it appears as only yesterday
that such glorious outfits were commonplace
on most race circuits

179 [*Left*] The first New Imperials built at
the turn of the century were bad enough that it
was said they could not even be given away.
No more news of New Imps then until 1910
when with the introduction of a lightweight
model, having two speeds and a countershaft
and selling so well, the company's future was
assured.

Keen adherents of the 'Racing improves the
Breed' policy, the company entered their
machines in sporting events from the end of
the Great War until 1936. It must not pass
unnoticed, however, that during this period
many very worthwhile road-going machines
were produced. Note, for example, the range
of worthy models for 1920 and, indeed,
M Mathieu's commendation!

180 [*Above*] In a period when the rather scruffy sidecar outfit would serve as both a grass track and road racing device, one man had different ideas. Possibly the most successful of all British pre-war sidecar road racing stars, Arthur Horton, is seen here with passenger Les Seals as they work the big 596cc Norton outfit at Crystal Palace, 25th June 1938. Horton realised only too well that if races were to be won a truly professional approach, both in machine preparation and human skill, would be prime requirements. It all paid off, as the saying goes, with countless wins at Donington and Crystal Palace, to say nothing of the brilliant Horton/Seals victory in the Swiss Grand Prix of '38.

Horton favoured retention of the plunger rear suspension, while others preferred to race 'solid'. Incidentally, the sidecar was home made! Today, Arthur Horton runs a very large chain of betting shops in London. He last appeared in racing sidecar events in the early post-war period

181 [*Above right*]   Italian Grand Prix, Monza, 14th September 1950. This magnificent action shot depicts British sidecar ace Eric Oliver literally bending his Norton/ Watsonian outfit round the cobbled surface of one of Monza's several bends. Oliver's passenger, believed to be Lorenzo Dobelli [local talent] appears to be shaking a clenched fist at some other runners, but has not neglected his vital duty as sidecar crew man two, and has applied considerable pressure to the outfit's wheel casing, thus forcing the sidecar wheel to remain in contact with terra firma. Possibly the greatest sidecar racer of all time, Eric Oliver had much experience of solo machines, in both pre and post-war years, although he will be remembered by all race enthusiasts as King of the Charioteers. It would be wise to add that Oliver won the Italian, and was four times world sidecar champion, and later pioneer of the kneeler outfit that today is used by all three wheeler racing men. All the old mastery is there when Eric appears as guest on some VMCC race days

182 [*Right*] All we are told is that 16 year old Rebecca Lee of New South Wales, Australia, delivered milk each morning before leaving for school. That was in 1946. One wonders just what Miss Lee is doing today.

The Ariel in the picture is possibly a 600cc version of the side valve range, designed mainly for hauling a sidecar or float, as we see here.

Fulfilling a definite role, it is indeed odd that no side valve motorcycle suited for hard slogging is any longer produced by any motorcycle manufacturer. Fashions change, however, and with renewed interest in single cylinder power units, who knows, we may yet witness the renaissance of the meaty side valve jobs. Additionally, the sidecar, out of favour for some years, is becoming popular once more. One hopes that its revival will be treated seriously and not in a gimmicky way, as there is a present tendency to do with many otherwise sensible things

INDEX OF PHOTOGRAPHS

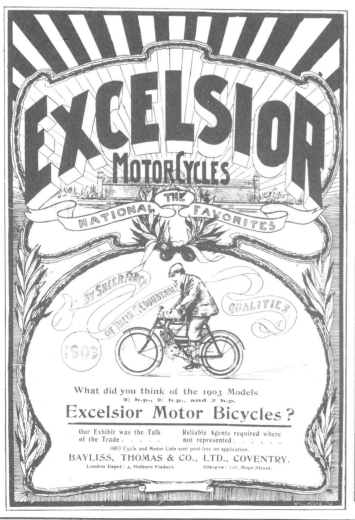